"McKenna's deft exploration of various aspects of *Big Wednesday* reveals it to be far more than a cult surfing movie. This wide-ranging study not only provides an astute account of the film's initial failure and eventual reappraisal but also focuses productively on how it works as an overtly sentimental male melodrama about the loss of youthful friendship."

– **Martin Shingler**, independent scholar, freelance writer, editor and researcher.

"This is an impressively wide-ranging, carefully researched and engagingly written study of an oft neglected movie classic. In addition to an illuminating analysis of *Big Wednesday* and of the film's making, marketing and reception, the book offers a compelling account of the importance and evolution of surf culture, and a wealth of new insights into the careers of its maverick writer-director, John Milius, and its three leading men. All this is presented with detailed references to key debates in Film Studies and to significant trends in Hollywood cinema since the 1960s."

– **Peter Krämer**, author of *American Graffiti: George Lucas, the New Hollywood and the Baby Boom Generation (2023) and co-editor of The Hollywood Renaissance: Revisiting American Cinema's Most Celebrated Era* (2018).

"McKenna deftly analyzes John Milius' *Big Wednesday*, as an under-appreciated film classic that culminates the New Hollywood renaissance. This is a multi-faceted cultural study that invigorates questions ranging from 'Is Milius' "bad boy" brand "chic fascism"?' to 'What is male melodrama?' that smartly links the 1978 movie to current anxieties."

– **Frederick Wasser**, Professor at Brooklyn College – CUNY.

Big Wednesday

This book provides an examination of *Big Wednesday* as an unconventional film that employs a mythic sensibility in its representation of the loss of youth and young manhood.

Critically and commercially unsuccessful on its original release, the coming-of-age, surf drama *Big Wednesday* (1978), has undergone a significant reappraisal. It is now considered not only an important contribution to youth cinema, but also the most important film that John Milius ever made. Over six chapters, the book considers questions of authorship, commerce, genre, stardom, and myth, and explores how these ideas intersect with the film's status as a significant youth movie and collectively how these ideas have contributed to its recent critical rehabilitation. In doing so, the book also provides a much-needed reassessment of an important and overlooked entry in the New Hollywood canon.

Exploring *Big Wednesday*'s subsequent resonance and relevance, this unique study will appeal to students and scholars in film studies, popular culture studies, youth studies, sociology, and media studies.

Mark McKenna is an Associate Professor in Film and Media Industries at Staffordshire University. His research interests are broadly focused on marketing and branding practices, media labour processes, and media policy and regulation strategy, and his work has explored these ideas in a range of contexts and from a number of different perspectives. He is the author of *Nasty Business: The Marketing and Distribution of the Video Nasties* and *Snuff*, and the co-editor of *Horror Franchise Cinema* (Routledge, 2021).

Cinema and Youth Cultures

Series Editors: Siân Lincoln and Yannis Tzioumakis

Cinema and Youth Cultures engages with well-known youth films from American cinema as well as the cinemas of other countries. Using a variety of methodological and critical approaches the series volumes provide informed accounts of how young people have been represented in film, while also exploring the ways in which young people engage with films made for and about them. In doing this, the Cinema and Youth Cultures series contributes to important and long-standing debates about youth cultures, how these are mobilized and articulated in influential film texts and the impact that these texts have had on popular culture at large.

American Graffiti
George Lucas, the New Hollywood and the Baby Boom Generation
Peter Krämer

Before Sunrise
Young Love on the Move
María del Mar Azcona and Celestino Deleyto

Rock around the Clock
Exploitation, Rock 'n' Roll and the Origins of Youth Culture
Yannis Tzioumakis and Siân Lincoln

Spider-Man: Into the Spider-Verse
Youth, Race, and the Hypertext
Charlie Michael

Big Wednesday
Lamenting Lost Youth in the New Hollywood
Mark McKenna

For more information about this series, please visit: https://www.routledge.com/Cinema-and-Youth-Cultures/book-series/CYC

Big Wednesday

Lamenting Lost Youth in the New Hollywood

Mark McKenna

LONDON AND NEW YORK

First published 2025
by Routledge
4 Park Square, Milton Park, Abingdon, Oxon OX14 4RN

and by Routledge
605 Third Avenue, New York, NY 10158

Routledge is an imprint of the Taylor & Francis Group, an informa business

British Library Cataloguing-in-Publication Data
A catalogue record for this book is available from the British Library

Library of Congress Cataloging-in-Publication Data
Names: McKenna, Mark, 1975- author
Title: Big Wednesday : lamenting lost youth in the new Hollywood / Mark McKenna.
Description: London ; New York : Routledge, 2025. |
Series: Cinema and youth cultures | Includes bibliographical references and index. |
Contents: Story telling in new Hollywood -- Friendship, innocence, and mythologized youth -- Resistance and incorporation in Californian surf culture -- Authorship and the star director -- Genere and the male melodrama -- Youthful archetypes and the transition to cult stardom.
Identifiers: LCCN 2024029413 (print) | LCCN 2024029414 (ebook) | ISBN 9780367178925 hardback | ISBN 9781032801117 paperback | ISBN 9780429058295 ebook
Subjects: Classification: LCC PN1997.B4464 M35 2025 (print) | LCC PN1997.B4464 (ebook) | DDC 791.43/72--dc23/eng/20240822
LC record available at https://lccn.loc.gov/2024029413
LC ebook record available at https://lccn.loc.gov/2024029414

ISBN: 978-0-367-17892-5 (hbk)
ISBN: 978-1-032-80111-7 (pbk)
ISBN: 978-0-429-05829-5 (ebk)

DOI: 10.4324/9780429058295

Typeset in Times New Roman
by Taylor & Francis Books

This is a book about friendship or, more specifically, it is a book about a film about friendship. I first encountered *Big Wednesday* in 1988 when it was broadcast as part of the BBC's cineaste series *Moviedrome*, a pioneering show in which Alex Cox curated cult content for an eager British audience. Even at that young age, something about the film resonated with me and the themes of friendship and loss that seemed so important and that were rendered on such a grand scale always stayed with me. Many years later when an opportunity came up to write a book for this series, *Big Wednesday* was my first choice.

Like many people with a young family, the pandemic severely impacted on my life and my work, but that process was derailed even further when I lost one of my oldest friends to suicide. The book then took on a far greater significance, becoming a marker of my own friendships and a measure of what has been lost and gained in the decades through which we had known each other. As I worked through these emotions and finally began to see the book come together, I lost another of my closest friends unexpectedly and then, towards the end, against all odds, another.

I am still processing what these three losses mean and I imagine it will take a very long time before I can fully reconcile the feelings that I have about losing three of the most important friends that I have ever known. Stu was always fascinated by numerology and he had a particular fondness for the number 9, so I am sure that he would find some great cosmic significance in the fact that *Big Wednesday* follows the fortunes of three friends; that in the production of the film, three friends collaborated on a unique profit sharing cooperative that still frames how the film is discussed; and that over the course of writing this book, I have lost three friends. Whatever significance he would have found, my little book about a film about friendship has taken on a personal significance far greater than I ever could have imagined when I first began this project. I dedicate this book to them, and to quote *Big Wednesday*, this book is for our friends, 'for our friends, come hell or high water'.

Steven Tate	Stuart Reilly	Johnson Cleugh
05/05/75–24/06/19	05/08/70–24/02/23	08/07/74–21/05/23

Contents

	List of Figures	x
	Series Editors' Introduction	xii
	Acknowledgements	xiv
	Introduction	1
1	Storytelling in New Hollywood	5
2	Friendship, Innocence, and Mythologised Youth	16
3	Resistance and Incorporation in Californian Surf Culture	36
4	Authorship and the Star Director	53
5	Genre and the Male Melodrama	69
6	Youthful Archetypes and the Transition to Cult Stardom	87
	Epilogue	110
	Bibliography	113
	Index	124

Figures

1.1 Milius' friendship with Lucas and Spielberg exemplified the spirit of youthful enthusiasm in the New Hollywood, seen here in a script review meeting (left to right, Spielberg, Milius and Lucas) (screengrab from *Milius* [2013]) 7

2.1 In crafting the conclusion to *Big Wednesday* Milius invokes the climactic scene of Sam Peckinpah's *The Wild Bunch* (1969) 25

2.2 Frames as thresholds: sub-framing in *Big Wednesday* as an homage to John Ford's *The Searchers* (1956) 30

3.1 A subculture within a subculture: white youths perform Nazi salutes while heading to the beach in California to surf, 1961 (screengrab from *Waves Apart* [2022]) 41

3.2 Screenshot of Edison's *Hawaiian Islands* (1906), a film that is aesthetically close to Booth's category of Pure surfing films 46

4.1 A photograph of Milius in his office that captures some of the performativity of the 'Zen-Anarchist', surrounded by iconic symbols of war and surfing (image reproduced from *Milius* [2013]) 62

6.1 Gary Busey, seen here in his greatest critical success, *The Buddy Holly Story* (1978), and then in *Celebrity Big Brother* (2014) in a scene that captures some of the excess for which he has latterly become known. 97

6.2 William Katt, as the romantic lead with curly blond ringlets, seen here in *Carrie* (1976) and as Ralph Hinkley, the *Greatest American Hero* (1982), a role that encapsulates Katt's qualities as the quintessential 'Good Joe' 99

6.3 From youthful archetype and embodiment of Klapp's 'Pin-Up' in *Big Wednesday* to a fallen star whose private life overshadowed the promise of his early career (image from 'The Tragic Demise & Death of Jan-Michael Vincent', *Golden Rewind* [2024]) 104
6.4 Gary Busey, William Katt, Lee Purcell, Darrell Fetty (Waxer), and Jan-Michael Vincent on the convention circuit at The Hollywood Show, capitalising on rekindled interest in *Big Wednesday.* Image reproduced courtesy of The Hollywood Show. 106

Series Editors' Introduction

Despite the high visibility of youth films in the global media marketplace (especially since the 1980s, when Conglomerate Hollywood realised that such films were not only strong box office performers but also the starting point for ancillary sales in other media markets as well as for franchise building), academic studies that focused specifically on such films were slow to materialise. Arguably the most important factor behind academia's reluctance to engage with youth films was a (then) widespread perception within the film and media studies communities that such films held little cultural value and significance, and therefore were not worthy of serious scholarly research and examination. Just like the young subjects they represented, whose interests and cultural practices have been routinely deemed transitional and transitory, so were the films that represented them perceived as fleeting and easily digestible, destined to be forgotten quickly, as soon as the next youth film arrived in cinema screens a week later.

Under these circumstances, and despite a small number of pioneering studies in the 1980s and early 1990s, the field of 'youth film studies' did not really start blossoming and attracting significant scholarly attention until the 2000s and in combination with similar developments in cognate areas such as 'girl studies'. However, because of the paucity of material in the previous decades, the majority of these new studies in the 2000s focused primarily on charting the field and therefore steered clear of long, in-depth examinations of youth films or was exemplified by edited collections that chose particular films to highlight certain issues to the detriment of others. In other words, despite providing often wonderfully rich accounts of youth cultures as these have been captured by key films, these studies could not have possibly dedicated sufficient space to engage with more than just a few key aspects of youth films.

In more recent (post-2010) years a number of academic studies started delimiting their focus and therefore providing more space for in-depth examinations of key types of youth films, such as slasher films and biker films or examining youth films in particular historical periods. From that point on, it was a matter of time for the first publications that focused exclusively on key youth films from a number of perspectives to appear (*Mamma Mia! The Movie, Twilight*, and *Dirty Dancing* were among the first films to receive this treatment). Conceived primarily as edited collections, these studies provided a multifaceted analysis of these films, focusing on such issues as the politics of representing youth, the stylistic and narrative choices that characterise these films and the extent to which they are representative of a youth cinema, the ways these films address their audiences, the ways youth audiences engage with these films, the films' industrial location, and other relevant issues.

It is within this increasingly maturing and expanding academic environment that the **Cinema and Youth Cultures** volumes arrive, aiming to consolidate existing knowledge, provide new perspectives, apply innovative methodological approaches, offer sustained and in-depth analyses of key films, and therefore become the 'go to' resource for students and scholars interested in theoretically informed, authoritative accounts of youth cultures in film. As editors, we have tried to be as inclusive as possible in our selection of key examples of youth films by commissioning volumes on films that span the history of cinema, including the silent film era; that portray contemporary youth cultures as well as ones associated with particular historical periods; that represent examples of mainstream and independent cinema; that originate in American cinema and the cinemas of other nations; that attracted significant critical attention and commercial success during their initial release and that were 'rediscovered' after an unpromising initial critical reception. Together these volumes are going to advance youth film studies while also being able to offer extremely detailed examinations of films that are now considered significant contributions to cinema and our cultural life more broadly.

We hope readers will enjoy the series.

Siân Lincoln and Yannis Tzioumakis
Cinema and Youth Cultures series editors

Acknowledgements

I would like to thank both Siân and Yannis as series editors, and Natalie Foster at Routledge for their patience and support while I was writing this book. For the reasons detailed above, the process took far longer than expected; however, I think the extra time allowed me to streamline my ideas and better reflect my ambitions for the book, mapping these back to the goals of the series. I'd would like to thank Amanda Milius for our conversations when I was first beginning this process; my colleagues Sharon Coleclough, Stephen Griffiths, Rachel Heeley, and Rob Marsden for their continued support while I was writing this book; Eddie Falvey for helping me track down some early issues of *Film Comment*; Dave Fennell for the scan of *Surfing* magazine; Gary Needham for alerting me to the work of Paul Alcuin Siebenand; and Joan Ormrod, who was kind enough to share her fantastic work on *Big Wednesday*. Thanks to the staff at the Margaret Herrick Library, University of California–Berkeley, and the University of California–Santa Cruz who provided archival assistance during the pandemic. Thanks to Troy Lewis and The Hollywood Show for permission to reprint their fantastic image of the friends together. My thanks to my old friends, Will Crosby, who kept encouraging me to finish the book, and to William Proctor, whose wealth of knowledge and memories of a childhood spent at the beach are as vivid as my own. Both of you helped me, as did Gwyn Thomas, giving me the occasional appropriately timed kick in the right direction. My thanks also to Kelly and Sylvia for reminding me of the importance of this book. I thank you all for your support. A huge thank you my production editor at Routledge, Christina O'Brien Thornton, for accommodating my many requests and for making the production process so easy and straightforward. Finally, my thanks, as always, to Martin and Sarah, my long-suffering peer reviewers. Thank you for your feedback on earlier drafts and to Sarah for tolerating my incessant chattering about John Milius and the importance of *Big Wednesday* for 4+ years. To anyone I have forgotten, this is not a reflection on you or your contribution to the project, but rather my failing memory – my thanks always.

Introduction

Big Wednesday (1978) is a coming-of-age drama set against the backdrop of 1960s and 1970s Californian surf culture. Written by John Milius and Dennis Aaberg and directed by Milius, the film is a semi-autobiographical fictionalised account of their experiences growing up in Malibu. It is also the most personal film that Milius has ever made and remains an anomaly in the career of a director whose work has otherwise been preoccupied with the violence of great men. In *Big Wednesday*, those great men are pitted against the sea and the violence replaced with a melodramatic celebration of lost youth.[1] The film features what was, at that time at least, some of the most dynamic and dramatic footage of surfing ever captured on film. However, while surfing figures centrally in the film's narrative and played a pivotal role in the film's rehabilitation after a lukewarm original reception, it would be a mistake to categorise *Big Wednesday* as simply a 'surf movie'. Surfing merely provides the stage for a film that is primarily concerned with the importance of friendship. From its opening voiceover narration to its closing theme, *Big Wednesday* is a lamentation to lost youth and the friends that were found there. Milius has said that the film is about 'the loss of aristocracy, the end of an era, the passing of a more innocent time to a more corrupt and complex one' and that 'all growing is the passing of innocence'. He has compared it to John Ford's *How Green Was My Valley* (1941), suggesting that at its core it is a film about 'friendship and the value of friendship' (Thompson 1976: 10). The film has been described as grandiose and pretentious (Cox 1988), and it is perhaps because of this that it was unsuccessful on its original release.

However, in the intervening years, the film has undergone a significant reappraisal, garnering a cult following with each successive generation to finally being considered by many as Milius' finest moment. The film would find a new audience on home video, then DVD and Blu-ray, and has become a favourite at midnight screenings

DOI: 10.4324/9780429058295-1

at movie festivals – most recently playing to sell-out crowds at Quentin Tarantino's repertory theatre, The New Beverly Cinema in Hollywood (Purcell 2022). The film is an important entry in the career of a significant, but often overlooked director during what is arguably the most celebrated period in contemporary film history. However, the road to redemption for *Big Wednesday* has not been straightforward and, as this book will explore, the rehabilitation of the film has been influenced by a number of different factors, not least the commercialisation of surfing during that period. Over six chapters, the book will adopt a range of different approaches with a view to understanding the film's contribution to youth culture, a contribution that is the product of an eclectic mix of factors that involve questions of authorship, genre, stardom, myth, and the ongoing commercialisation of surfing. And while the film's distinct approach to Californian surf culture and the journey from youth to adulthood originally found a muted response with cinema audiences, the film has more recently been rehabilitated, and the volume examines some of the reasons behind this.

As a means of anchoring that discussion, the book begins not with a narrative analysis of *Big Wednesday* itself, but instead with an introduction to Milius, exploring his place in the history of New Hollywood and considering what a story that is often told about the production of *Big Wednesday* can tell us about the director. That story concerns Milius' own friendship with Steven Spielberg and George Lucas during the 1970s, when the three young filmmakers were just beginning their career in Hollywood. It charts how their idealism and male camaraderie were challenged as the realities of working in a competitive industry derailed their youthful optimism. This chapter documents the different paths followed by each of the friends and the obstacles that this put in the way of their friendship, which in some ways is foreshadowed by the narrative of *Big Wednesday.* Chapter 2 offers a close reading of *Big Wednesday*, and through an analysis of structure and plot, narrative and themes, and style and aesthetics, will consider how the film constructs ideas of youth and reflects back on them as the narrative progresses. *Big Wednesday* is an unusual film in many respects, not least because it switches lead protagonist midway through the film. This chapter will explore these elements and interrogate a claim that is often levied against the film, namely that it is grandiose and pretentious.

Chapter 3 presents *Big Wednesday* as a reaction to the 'surf boom' of the 1960s and a point of resistance against the commercialisation of surfing seen in the popular beach party movies of American International Pictures and the surf rock sound of Jan and Dean. However, rather than consider this as an isolated moment, it presents the surf boom as part of a longer process of commodification and a wave of commercialisation stretching back to turn of the century Hawaii and a tourism drive that initiated the export and commercialisation of the sport in the first place. It will examine how these early attempts to capitalise on the pastime created pockets in which a Californian subculture emerged and began to thrive, popularising the image of the surfer, which was then exported globally as arguably the most identifiable image of Californian youth culture. Building on the work of Timothy Corrigan and Robert E. Kapsis, Chapter 4 explores the ways in which Milius parlayed his auteur status into a kind of stardom, establishing the parameters of a personality that would come to define his subsequent career and function as an authorial brand. It will consider how this brand initially benefited Milius, but ultimately began to falter when his larger-than-life machismo fell from favour with the critics and the cinemagoing public. With the intentional excess of Milius seemingly at odds with the tone and spirit of *Big Wednesday*, his most autobiographical film, this chapter will explore the performativity that underpins this public persona, and consider it an elaborate construction, an aspect often ignored by critics. In doing so, this chapter seeks to understand the film not as an outlier in his career as some suggest, but as the film that most accurately reflects the man.

Chapter 5 offers a brief history of the male melodrama, charting its evolution from the teen films of the 1950s, and titles like *Rebel Without a Cause* (Ray, 1955), through to the present day, and the commercial success of sports dramas, such as *Creed III* (Jordan, 2023). This account provides context for considering the specific difficulties involved in bringing a film like *Big Wednesday* to the market in the 1970s. In doing this, the chapter will also evaluate the commercial limitations of genre as a method for film classification, arguing that audiences often bring different associations to films when navigating what are often quite arbitrary film categories. Finally, Chapter 6 explores the role that the film's stars, Gary Busey, William Katt, and Jan-Michael Vincent, have all played in the reappraisal of the film. It will survey how the established star image of each of the actors differs and deviates from the youthful archetypes that defined their earlier stardom (partly established in *Big Wednesday*), and how these ideas map to a taxonomy first developed by Orrin Edgar Klapp in the 1950s. It will then consider the limitations of that taxonomy in assessing the complexity of star images, using this template as a starting point to understand the evolution of the actors from youthful archetypes to cult stars, and consider how these discursive narratives mirror the trajectory of their characters in *Big Wednesday*.

As is clear from these brief chapter descriptions, the book takes some of the most established concepts from film, media, and cultural studies, and uses *Big Wednesday* as a vehicle through which to explore them. Considering themes of authorship, genre, stardom, narrative, and commerce, the book examines how each of these concepts has been utilised in efforts to provide a critical understanding and appreciation of the film, to determine its place in the history of the New Hollywood, and to examine the ways it represents youth on screen.

Note

1 Milius has said that '*Big Wednesday* was violent, but there were no guns. It was just a man and a wave, and that's scary' (Gallagher 1989: 179–80).

1 Storytelling in New Hollywood

In the late 1960s and early 1970s, a vibrant new generation of young filmmakers emerged to challenge the studio-driven paradigm that had governed Hollywood throughout the classical period. This shift heralded an unprecedented era of creativity, led by an impressive cadre of young, and largely university-educated directors like Francis Ford Coppola, Martin Scorsese, Brian De Palma, Steven Spielberg, George Lucas, Paul Schrader, and John Milius. Affectionately known as 'the Movie Brats', the group were steeped in the grammar, history, and traditions of film and, for a brief moment, they wrested the power away from the studios and, in doing so, reshaped the cinematic landscape for generations to come.

In many contemporary histories of the New Hollywood, John Milius is presented as a peripheral figure, a footnote in the careers of his extraordinarily successful friends, George Lucas and Steven Spielberg. However, his contribution to the cinema of the period is considerable. As a writer, he is responsible for three of the most iconic monologues in cinematic history: Clint Eastwood as notoriously ruthless San Francisco street cop *Dirty Harry* (Siegel, 1971) Callahan, spitting through gritted teeth, 'Do I feel lucky? Well, do you, punk?'; Robert Duval as Lieutenant Colonel Bill Kilgore in *Apocalypse Now* (Coppola, 1979) striding over the remnants of a captured Vietnamese peninsula pausing to remark 'I love the smell of napalm in the morning'; and a glassy-eyed Robert Shaw as grizzled ancient mariner Captain Quint in *Jaws* (1976) recounting with horror the sinking of the USS Indianapolis: 'So, eleven hundred men went into the water. Three hundred and sixteen men come out, the sharks took the rest, June the 29th, 1945'.[1] As a director, his work has been said to belong to 'the great American tradition of larger-than-life narrative filmmaking, best embodied by John Ford, Howard Hawks, and John Huston' (Gallagher 1989: 169), and collectively, his films have explored themes of

DOI: 10.4324/9780429058295-2

chivalry, honour, loyalty and love, through the lens of masculine conflict. His work frequently returns to explore the actions of uncompromising men, in difficult situations, dolling out, or responding to, violence, and, because of this, they have been read as a reflection of his own conservative politics with films like *Dillinger* (1973), *Conan the Barbarian* (1982), and *Red Dawn* (1984) seen to typify this oeuvre.

In the early 1970s, Milius was at the vanguard of the group of writers and directors who were poised to shake up Hollywood. In 1973, the *New York Times* dubbed him Hollywood's 'enfant terrible' (Weiler 1973: 31) and Burr Snider called him the 'high priest of High Media' (1973), suggesting that 'in the palmy, balmy little community nestled between the San Fernando Valley and the sea, the place where our collective visions are tacky-tailored to meet shooting schedules and our grandest fantasies ground out in ninety-minute segments', Milius was 'just about the hottest item going' (1973). With his friends, Lucas and Spielberg, Milius helped to redefine contemporary cinema, and while he has enjoyed varying degrees of success, with occasional moments of brilliance in which he has lived up to the promise of those early reviews, the quality of his work has often been overshadowed by the weight of his public persona (see Chapter 4 for a detailed examination of this). Deliberately excessive and unquestionably provocative, much of this persona is articulated for effect. But over time as this image was remediated through the press it became difficult to separate fact from fiction and determine where the real Milius finished and his performative persona began. He quickly garnered a reputation for difficult and unpredictable behaviour and, despite possessing an incredible talent, particularly as a writer, he gradually fell from favour with the studios who were unable or unwilling to tolerate his excessive behaviour. In many ways, this is Milius' greatest creation, a mythic exaggerated persona that has become central to how we understand the man and his work. This persona served as the basis for John Goodman's comedic, Vietnam-obsessed, gun-toting, bowler Walter Sobchak in the Coen brothers' cult classic *The Big Lebowski* (1998), but he has also served as the inspiration for the Milius authored, John Belushi performed, Captain Kelso in *1941* (1979) and, ironically, the surf rock hating John Milner in *American Graffiti* (1973).

The success of this persona came at considerable cost to the director, who insists that the popular perception of him and his politics has ensured that he has been blacklisted for the better part of his professional life, just 'as surely as any writer was blacklisted back in the 1950s' (D'Arcy 2001). While this claim is contested by Alfio Leotta, who argues instead that 'his decline was more likely the consequence of an unfortunate combination of illnesses and commercial failure rather than an actual political blacklist' (2019: x), the persona and the politics have undoubtedly left an indelible stain that overshadows any discussion of the director and his work. Those reports that do consider Milius either focus on the hyperbolic story of 'the craziest man in Hollywood' (Green 2013) or reduce him to a footnote to the careers of his extraordinarily successful friends, Lucas and Spielberg.

One of these footnotes concerns the production of *Big Wednesday* and the formation of a unique cinematic cooperative through which Lucas, Spielberg, and Milius would swap profit participation points, allowing each to earn a percentage of the gross from the other's films. It was as a result of this agreement that Lucas and Milius came to own a percentage of *Close Encounters of the Third Kind* (Spielberg, 1977); that Spielberg and Milius came to own a percentage of *Star Wars* (Lucas, 1977); and that Lucas and Spielberg came to own a percentage of *Big Wednesday*. In an interview with the *New York Times* in 1978, Milius described how his friends would often collaborate on each other's work (see Figure 1.1) and while much of this was simply delivered in the spirit of friendship, in the case of major rewrites or other substantial aid, they would give one another a small percentage of the profits from each other's movies in recognition of the services rendered (quoted in Lindsey 1978: SM3). As Milius explained, 'one point in a picture like "*Star Wars*" can mean a lot', but this was never the motivation (quoted in Lindsey 1978: SM3).

Figure 1.1 Milius' friendship with Lucas and Spielberg exemplified the spirit of youthful enthusiasm in the New Hollywood, seen here in a script review meeting (left to right, Spielberg, Milius and Lucas) (screengrab from *Milius* [2013])

Star Wars would go on to redefine popular cinema, and *Close Encounters* would become Columbia Pictures' most successful film to date. Spielberg felt certain that by combining the oceanic appeal of *Jaws* (Spielberg, 1975), with the 1960s nostalgia that had been so central to the success of Lucas' *American Graffiti, Big Wednesday* was sure to be a hit and guaranteed an audience far beyond the marginal crowds that they could expect for their little sci-fi movies (Fleming Jnr. 2010). He was wrong. Released in the wake of *Saturday Night Fever* (Badham, 1977), *Big Wednesday* failed to find an audience and vanished without a trace, taking only $4.5 million at the box office on an estimated budget of $11,000,000 (Leotta 2018: 69).

This is a story that is often reproduced in anecdotal histories of the period and is typically recounted to illustrate the unprecedented success of *Close Encounters of the Third Kind* and *Star Wars* and, by way of comparison, the catastrophic failure of Milius and his passion project *Big Wednesday*. However, most films would fall short economically when measured against the behemoth that *Star Wars* became, and while Spielberg and Lucas would both experience similar disappointments in the 1980s,[2] the failure of *Big Wednesday* would cast a long shadow over Milius and his career. He would later say of the failure that 'it was like committing a political crime, worse than a regular crime' (Fleming Jnr. 2010). Some accounts, like that of Lucas' biographer John Baxter, get swept up in the romanticism of the deal, arguing that the collective was 'in a spirit of comradeship that harked back to the earliest ideals of New Hollywood' (2000: 247). However, the majority, even those that are broadly supportive of Milius and *Big Wednesday* (see Fleming Jnr. [2010]) cannot help but dwell upon the devastating failure that *Big Wednesday* became.

Peter Biskind uses the point trading agreement with Milius as an example of the foolishness and inexperience of Lucas, suggesting that while Willard Huyck, Gloria Katz, Harrison Ford, Carrie Fisher, Mark Hamill, and sound designer Ben Burtt all received profit participation points, the exchange with Milius was a step too far. Biskind even suggests that once the failure of *Big Wednesday* became clear, Lucas tried to renege on his part of the deal and asked Milius for his points back (Biskind 1998: 340), clearly less invested 'in the spirit of comradeship' once he had a runaway hit on his hands. When Spielberg was asked to comment on the outcome of the deal, he reportedly said that 'we only did that once, and it worked out better for some than others' (Fleming Jnr. 2010), while Lucas has similarly joked that he's 'still waiting to see that *Big Wednesday* money' (Lucas 2013).

Milius has refused to comment on how much he made from his stake in *Close Encounters* and *Star Wars,* but he has gone as far as to say that it helped him pay for his divorce, a romance that he said inspired the comparatively gentle tone of *Big Wednesday* in the first place (Segaloff 2021: 44). While the financial disagreements between the friends work to dull some of the romanticism of Baxter's celebratory reading of the exchange, the more critical accounts can be seen to do three things: first, they work to minimise Milius' place in the development of the New Hollywood, by casting him as a peripheral figure at a moment when he was actually considered the 'scout leader' of the group;[3] second, they suggest that disagreements over the exchange became a source of conflict between the friends that would lead to the dissolution of the group, when in reality they remained close friends and would continue to work together for many years to come (Milius provided the story for *1941* and script revisions for *Indiana Jones and the Temple of Doom* [Spielberg, 1984]) and much later, *Saving Private Ryan* (Spielberg, 1998); and third, they suggest that Milius' career never really recovered from the disappointment of *Big Wednesday,* when his greatest successes still lay ahead of him. While none of these things are really true, each works to erode Milius' contribution to the cinema of the period and imagines him an outlier in the history of the New Hollywood when he was one of its earliest exponents.

In many ways, much of this minimisation can be attributed to the meteoric rise of his friends and the production of an unprecedented body of work that accounts for some of the most successful films of all time. It is difficult to imagine the 1980s, or indeed the film industry today, without the immeasurable impact and influence of George Lucas and Steven Spielberg. Together and apart, they redefined popular film and, in the case of the former, created much of the digital infrastructure on which the contemporary industry is now built. Through his companies Lucasfilm, LucasArts and Industrial Light and Magic, Lucas achieved a studio-like level of control over the production process, while through THX, itself a subsidiary of Lucasfilm, he developed what became the industry standard for high fidelity audio/visual reproduction for movie theatres. Even Spielberg, though most often celebrated for his creative accomplishments, has comfortably moved beyond the role of writer/director to establish himself as a contemporary movie mogul, first in collaboration with Kathleen Kennedy[4] and Frank Marshall at Amblin Entertainment, and then in partnership with Jeffrey Katzenberg and David Geffen with DreamWorks SKG. With grosses adjusted for inflation, Spielberg has directed three of the top 20 grossing films of all time: *Jaws, E.T. the Extra-Terrestrial*

(1982) and *Jurassic Park* (1993), while Lucas directed the second most profitable film of all time, *Star Wars: Episode IV – A New Hope* (1977), serving as producer on a further three films in that top 20 list: *Star Wars: Episode V – The Empire Strikes Back* (Kershner, 1980), *Star Wars: Episode VI – Return of the Jedi* (Marquand, 1983), and *Star Wars: Episode I – The Phantom Menace* (1999), directing the last as well as being creative consultant on a fourth, *Star Wars: Episode VII – The Force Awakens* (Abrams, 2015). Together they steered Hollywood away from the auteurist cinema of the 1970s, of which they and Milius were originally a part, toward the blockbuster era of the 1980s and, in doing so, radically transformed the business of film. However, creative accomplishments aside, the position they occupy within the industry has as much to do with their business acumen as it does with creativity, and while undoubtedly more restrained than Milius, it would be a mistake to imagine their personae as organic and authentic. These are mediated identities and the result of a deliberate, strategic, and carefully curated brand management that has seen the pair dominate the film industry for almost five decades.

Providing some measure of that is an incident that took place in 1984 in which Lucas, Spielberg, and Milius found themselves embroiled in a debate about what constituted an appropriate level of violence for films aimed at a predominantly youth market – Lucas and Spielberg for *Indiana Jones and the Temple of Doom*, and Milius for *Red Dawn* (Antunes 2017; Kendrick 2009). While these debates would lead to the introduction of the PG-13 rating, how the friends negotiated these criticisms and their involvement and influence over the structural frameworks governing film, tells us much – not just about their shifting stock in Hollywood, but also about the popular perception of them and the markedly different brands that they had come to embody. James Russell has argued that 'Spielberg's style and thematic preoccupations are, in effect, the means through which he acquires a distinct market value – which is to say, they help establish a brand. In fact, Spielberg's personal brand remains particularly well defined – he has focused on depicting and addressing children and families' (Russell 2017: 47). However, while Russell cites the textual qualities that have undoubtedly contributed to our understanding of the Spielberg brand, these associations also help to define his extratextual persona, creating a star image of the director as the quiet and thoughtful all-American, baseball cap wearing, baby boomer with a Peter Pan complex.

Similarly, Lucas' association with technology has typically seen him cast as a bespectacled socially awkward nerd, more comfortable with the technology that became so fundamental to his success, than to interactions with the press or public. The success of both of these images contributed to a perception of both men as inoffensive and benevolent, a belief that disguises much of the strategic jostling for ownership that helped to secure their auteur status in the 1980s, a decade in which Lucas did not direct a single film.[5] Over the course of the decade, both Lucas and Spielberg secured their authorial status through a series of high-profile court cases that helped to assert the cultural, creative and commercial value of their names and, therefore, their brands. These range from attempts to assert propriety control over entire genres, to warring with the Directors Guild of America over who gets authorial credit. However, it is their interactions with the Motion Picture Association of America around the introduction of the PG-13 certificate that gives an incredibly clear insight into the legalistic wranglings that took place behind the scenes and that helped Lucas and Spielberg assert creative control over the industry, while leaving Milius pilloried as a pariah.

A Discursive Separation

By the early 1980s, Lucas and Spielberg had effectively become modern day movie moguls. However, the true measure of their reach and influence would not be felt until 1984 and the release of *Indiana Jones and the Temple of Doom*, and the Joe Dante directed, Spielberg produced *Gremlins. Temple of Doom* presented a very specific challenge for the ratings board in terms of its depiction of violence and, alongside the Spielberg produced *Poltergeist*, which had been released two years earlier, found itself at the centre of a growing debate.[6] Filipa Antunes suggests that although both were considered to be controversial films, debates around them were tempered by the perception of them as 'family-friendly' films, 'raising questions not about suitability in general but about suitability specifically in relation to small children, thus suggesting impending segmentation of the concept of childhood (2017: 29). In contrast, debates surrounding the release of *Gremlins* centred on the suitability of the film for an audience of children and the belief that it was 'closer to horror than a family film', inspiring debates about 'the viability of horror for a child audience, particularly under the PG classification' (36).

The combined effect of *Gremlins* and *Indiana Jones and the Temple of Doom* led to a series of complaints from parents that 'some scenes were simply too intense for young children' (Parker 2017). However, rather than reclassify the films as 15-certificate and therefore only suitable for an older audience, these debates would lead to the development of a new category. The film rating system had remained largely unchanged since its formation in 1968 and there was little desire for change from the long serving president Jack Valenti who, when interviewed in 1984, said 'I was opposed to any change in the ratings system, I think it's a fragile system and the insertion of more categories is not needed. I thought the PG itself was a sufficient warning but so many of my peers in the business have taken an opposite view that I decided to lead this movement rather than to follow it' (quoted in Parker 2017). However, while Valenti may have wanted to claim ownership over the initiative, Spielberg suggests that because he created the problem (through his involvement with *Poltergeist, Gremlins*, and *Indiana Jones and the Temple of Doom*), he provided the solution (Associated Press 2004). According to Spielberg, he went to Valenti and argued that they needed 'a rating between R and PG, because so many films were falling into a netherworld [...] of unfairness. Unfair that certain kids were exposed to *Jaws*, but also unfair that certain films were restricted, that kids who were 13, 14, 15 should be allowed to see'. Spielberg then claims that he suggested that they 'call it PG-13 or PG-14' and that Valenti 'determined that PG-13 would be the right age for that temperature of movie', thus changing the rating system forever (Windolf 2008). Spielberg's influence over the institutional frameworks governing film across the entirety of the United States cannot be understated here, and through this process he was able to preserve his credentials as the leading purveyor of family entertainment in the face of public anxiety and, in doing so, sidestep any criticisms of him and his work. Significantly, while Spielberg may have ushered in the new rating, neither of the films with which he was associated would be subject to new categorisation, and the first film to be released theatrically with the PG-13 certificate would be Milius' controversial war drama *Red Dawn*.

The release *of Red Dawn* helped to consolidate an image of the director that had been seeded years before and it is arguably here, in the convergence between the on- and off-screen, and in the collision between the dominant themes of his work and his larger-than-life public persona, that he begins to experience a professional decline. *Red Dawn* would irrevocably tie Milius to an image of jingoistic warmongering. Produced at the height of the Cold War, the film began as an anti-war narrative written by Kevin Reynolds as something akin to William Golding's *Lord of the Flies* (1954). However, when MGM executives wanted to turn the film into a 'teen Rambo' they enlisted Reagan's former secretary of defence, General Alexander Haig, as a consultant, and brought in Milius to rewrite and direct. He would spend much of preproduction in the Hudson Institute, a conservative think tank founded by Herman Kahn.

The film presents a dystopian future in which World War III begins when an alliance of the Soviet Union and Latin American states invades North America. When the town of Calumet, Colorado is annexed, a group of teenage guerillas known as the Wolverines leads the charge against the invasion. The film was a commercial success, taking almost $40 million at the domestic box office (*Red Dawn* n.d.), but much of this would be overshadowed by criticisms of its politics and from calls to censor a film that has since been called a 'Republican wet dream' (Arseneau 2007). According to the National Coalition on Television Violence, the film contained 134 acts of violence per hour and the *Guinness Book of Records* named it the most violent film ever made (Arseneau 2007), although in retrospect, the film seems remarkably tame and the criticisms levied against Milius somewhat unjustified. Milius has said that he took inspiration from French and Russian resistance stories – particularly the idea 'that they are not going to make a big difference, but the fact that they fought and died makes a symbolic difference' (quoted in Segaloff [2006]: 303), and the debt the film owes to respected films like *Battle for Algiers* (Pontecorvo, 1966) is evident throughout. That is not to say that the film is without its problems, and, as Alfio Leotta notes, Milius' romantic fascination with mountain men like Jedediah Smith and Jim Bridger (evident in his earlier script for *Jeremiah Johnson*) was given 'specific ideological connotations' through the filter of the Hudson Institute and the input of Haig and MGM's CEO Frank Yablans (Leotta 2018: 92).

However, as Peter Bart, at the time Senior Vice President for Production at MGM, explains, the politics presented on screen were not necessarily the politics of Milius. He recalls how the director came to him during production concerned that Haig and Yablans had railroaded the project and turned his film about the 'futility of war' into a 'flag-waving jingoistic movie' (Bart 1990: 113). They had, and when the film was released, critics roundly condemned the violence, jingoism and anti-communist sentiment, with much of that ire directed at Milius himself. While Leotta argues that 'the readings of *Red Dawn* as a merely anti-communist film […] fail to take into account the ideological complexity and ambiguity of the film (2018: 93), the controversy nevertheless consolidated the Milius 'brand'. The film cemented 'his reputation as a right-wing, pro-military, gun-toting director' (2018: 93), and a filmography that was 'characterised by violence, excess and contempt for liberalism and political correctness' (97). This was literally poles apart from his cautiously apolitical friends, Lucas and Spielberg.

While this can be understood as a discursive separation imposed upon the three by media coverage that located the friends in vastly different ideological spaces, it should also be understood as a deliberate strategy on the part of Lucas and Spielberg to move away from their now controversial friend. It is also a strategy that begins before the furore surrounding *Red Dawn*. In an interview on the set of *Raiders of the Lost Ark,* a film on which Milius performed numerous uncredited rewrites, Spielberg and Lucas recount the story of the decision to swap profit participation points, with one notable exception (Lucas and Spielberg 2022). In this retelling, Milius and his failed film about friendship, *Big Wednesday*, were no longer part of the story. Removed from that history, the story told was now about the profitable partnership between the *two* friends and the money that *they* had made in the business of film.

Conclusion

There is something significant about Lucas and Spielberg's decision to excise Milius from their retelling of the story, particularly since *Big Wednesday* is a film that celebrates the importance of friendship and youth. However, by 1984, the friends were no longer young – and the legalistic wranglings with the Motion Picture Association of America over what might constitute an appropriate level of violence for children, are perhaps the best illustration of the gulf that had grown between the ageing directors and their audience, but also the gulf that had grown between the friends. The idealised 'spirit of comradeship' celebrated by John Baxter as epitomising 'the earliest ideals of New Hollywood' (2000: 247), was gone, and while Milius' career would never again reach the commercial heights of *Red Dawn, Big Wednesday* would go on to find a new audience, first on video and then on DVD and Blu-ray. As the film acquired a cult status, the story of the three friends swapping profit participation points was remediated, giving the film an imprimatur of authenticity, and serving as an extratextual signature that the film was an authentic celebration of idealistic youth.

Notes

1 There are numerous conflicting accounts about who is ultimately responsible for authoring the Indianapolis speech.
2 Spielberg, the following year with *1941* (1979), and Lucas, in 1986 with *Howard the Duck* (1986) (a project that he initiated, and was directed by his USC classmate, Willard Huyck. They recovered more easily from the commercial failure of these films.

3 Spielberg described Milius as the group's 'scoutmaster', stating 'He's the one who will tell you to go on a trip and only take enough food, enough water for one day, and make you stay out longer than that. He's the one who says, "Be a man. I don't want to see any tears." He's a terrific raconteur, a wonderful story teller. John has more life than all the rest of us put together' (Lindsey 1978: SM3).

4 Kennedy's ascent was meteoric, beginning as Milius' personal assistant on the Spielberg directed Milius authored flop *1941* in 1979, to associate to Spielberg on *Raiders of the Lost Ark* in 1981, while in the same year she cofounded Amblin Entertainment with Spielberg and her future husband Frank Marshall. The following year she would serve as associate producer on *Poltergeist.*

5 While Spielberg's image remains largely intact, the public perception of Lucas changed irrevocably with his return to *Star Wars* and the release of the so called prequels. Not only were they seen to be inferior films to the original trilogy, but Lucas became embroiled in a series of high-profile lawsuits through which he attempted to assert ownership over fan creations. This discourse is most visible in the documentary *The People vs. George Lucas* (Philippe, 2010) and the song 'George Lucas Raped Our Childhood' (Hot Waffles, 2005).

6 While *Poltergeist* is clearly a horror film it was almost universally accepted as part of Spielberg's oeuvre and therefore a family film. Vincent Canby for the *New York Times* argued that *Poltergeist* was 'much closer in spirit and sensibility' to Spielberg's best films which have 'preserved the wonderment of childhood' (1982: C16), and therefore, was not as indebted to the horror film as a film like *Gremlins.*

2 Friendship, Innocence, and Mythologised Youth

Milius co-authored *Big Wednesday* with fellow surfer and journalist Denny Aaberg, inspired by a short story that Aaberg had published in a 1973 issue of *Tracks* Magazine entitled 'No Pants Mance' (Aaberg 1973: p. n/a). Though relatively short, the story sets up key scenes and sequences that would go on to feature prominently in *Big Wednesday* and presents a biographical sketch of the lives of a group of young surfers growing up in 1960s Malibu. Milius and Aaberg developed the story together with the idea of turning it into a novel that Milius called *Big Wednesday*, a title borrowed from a 1961 John Severson 16mm film that capitalised on the belief that all great surf days fall on a Wednesday.[1] They would abandon the book project to later develop it into a screenplay, spending a year ensuring that the script authentically captured their own experiences. Aaberg has said that 'It was a special time' when 'surfing was a brand new sport with its own aristocracy', while Milius added that 'we all knew it was special' and 'we knew it wouldn't last' (Warga 1977: N7Bla).

Big Wednesday is infused with this sense of wistful melancholy and, unlike other youth films, constructs ideas of youth and what it means to be young in the first act, with the remainder of the film reflecting on those ideas, as age inevitability moves the characters away from their idyllic youth. This chapter will explore how *Big Wednesday* engages in this process by considering how its structure and plot differ from the approaches generally favoured by Hollywood during this period, and how these elements work together to instil the narrative with a sense of mythic importance that simultaneously functions as a celebration and a lamentation to lost youth. It will examine how technical difficulties faced in the realisation of the film inform an aesthetic that borrows heavily from Ford and Peckinpah to create a sense of the ocean as the last mythic frontier, and how this mythic sensibility was always central to Milius' ambitions for the film.

DOI: 10.4324/9780429058295-3

Structure and Plot

Despite his significant contribution to cinema as a director, John Milius is most frequently remembered as a screenwriter, often as a contributing author to many of New Hollywood's greatest successes, an image that he has actively embraced and cultivated. In a characteristically provocative interview with Erik Bauer for *Creative Screenwriting* magazine, Milius argued that screenwriting was a mystical art form that could not, and indeed, should not, be deconstructed, condemning anyone that cared to try. He argued that he was 'never conscious of [his] screenplays having any acts' and insisted that he did not know what a character arc was, suggesting that this was all just 'bullshit' and that writers should just instinctively 'tell a story' (quoted in Bauer 2015). He credited his USC teacher, Irwin Blacker, for his unconventional approach, and suggested that Blacker did not concern himself with the structural components of screenwriting and that he was more concerned about his students' ability to tell 'a good yarn' (2015).

As appealing as it is to imagine Milius as an untrained outsider, a natural storyteller, educated by a similarly unconventional teacher, this in itself is 'a good yarn' that minimises Milius' formal education at one of the most prestigious film schools in the world. Indeed, Blacker's own book, *The Elements of Screenwriting,* prioritises structure above all else, citing celebrated screenwriter, producer and director Richard Brooks' belief that writing for the screen is explicitly dependent upon 'character, story and structure. Structure, structure, structure' (Blacker 1986: 16). While these ideas have a cultural value that contributes to the Milius brand and to the authorial function of the writer/director, his schooling at USC destabilises any claim as to a lack of knowledge, and the formal construction of *Big Wednesday* only serves to further complicate these ideas.

Big Wednesday is Shakespearian in its structure, presented over five acts, that are delivered through four sections and a coda that literally chart the shifting seasons of the characters' lives. While this kind of structure was unusual for Hollywood and a system that had typically favoured a three-act structure, it did have a long-established history in theatre. German playwright and novelist Gustav Freytag presents the model in his 1863 book *Pyramid in Die Technik des Dramas* (*Technique of the Drama* [2004]). Freytag details how this structure had served as the basis for William Shakespeare's tragedies *Macbeth* and *Romeo and Juliet*, amongst others. The structure builds upon Aristotle's dramatic theory detailed in *Poetics* (circa 335 B.C.) that suggested that a story must have a beginning, middle, and end, typically expressed in filmmaking as setup, confrontation, and resolution. Freytag's Pyramid adds two additional elements to this structure, beginning with 1. Exposition, 2. Rising Action, 3. Climax, 4. Falling Action, and concluding with 5. Denouement or Resolution. *Big Wednesday* maps perfectly onto this structure.

Typically, Act 1 functions as the set-up or introduction. It sets up the time and location of the story, it introduces the main characters, their interests, and their motivations, and it sets the stage for the narrative that will follow. In *Big Wednesday* this sequence is introduced as 'The South Swell (Summer 1962)' and is arguably the most important part of the film. It establishes the characters of Matt, Jack, and Leroy, and presents them as a kind of surfing royalty, and the summer of 1962 as an idyllic summer, free from the conflict, complications and challenges of adulthood. Typically, the first act would introduce an element that will later become the story's primary source of conflict, which is known as the inciting incident, or what Freytag calls the 'complication'. However, *Big Wednesday* is unconventional in that regard as there is no inciting incident, no moment of conflict that casts a long shadow over the rest of the film and serves as motivation for the characters. Instead, there is just an understated suggestion that the childhood idyl that has been presented throughout the first act may be coming to an end. The foreclosure of the pier and the displacement of their mentor, Bear, alongside the announcement of Peggy's pregnancy, are the most tangible indicators of the changing priorities that will come with impending adulthood and the challenges that they represent to youth.

In Act 2, or what Freytag's called the 'rising action', we begin to see the effect of those changes. Typically, the inciting incident would initiate a series of events that build towards the midpoint or climax in Act 3. This is often presented as a series of obstacles placed in the path of the protagonist that they must overcome as they attempt to reach their goals. In *Big Wednesday*, the absence of an inciting incident in Act 1 means that much of that action takes place in Act 2, introduced as 'The West Swell (Fall 1965)'. We see that the friends have begun to grow apart, Jack has taken on a role of some responsibility, working as a lifeguard at the beach, while Matt, now an alcoholic, is struggling with the pressures of adulthood. A car crash caused by a drunken Matt only further divides the two, but an opportunity for reconciliation happens when the pair are reunited for Bear's wedding, only to be divided again by the Vietnam draft. While Matt and Leroy and secondary characters like Waxer all actively try to avoid conscription, feigning madness, homosexuality, and disability, Jack enlists, and the friends find themselves separated again.

Unlike traditional narrative structures in which the climax comes at the end, in Freytag's Pyramid, the climax is simply one crescendo and a mid-point to a narrative that continues to develop. In Freytag's Pyramid, Act 3 signals a turning point in the story's structure, themes and ideas, and in *Big Wednesday* that takes place three years after Jack has left for Vietnam. Jack returns home only to find that his girlfriend, Sally, had moved on, and that his friend, Waxer, had died in Vietnam. Introduced as 'The North Swell (Winter 1968)', this third act is presented as a period of change in which the three friends, now older, reflect on the happiness of their youth. Matt is invited to a screening of a surfing documentary with the promise that it featured great footage of him in his heyday, to later find that he only plays a marginal role in the film. This act closes with the three friends reuniting at the cemetery to celebrate the life of their fallen friend.

Act 4, 'falling action', builds upon the events of the climax to move the film toward a natural narrative resolution, and while the name might suggest a winding down as the film reaches its inevitable conclusion, it is often in this fourth act that the story's central themes and narrative threads are pulled together. In *Big Wednesday* this is introduced as 'The Great Swell (Spring 1974)' and sees Matt trying to find his friends to let them know that a great swell is building. When he cannot find them, he goes to meet Bear at the remnants of the broken-down pier, where Bear used to work. He explains to an inconsolable Bear that he could not find his friends and tries to convince him to come home with him to get warm and have some soup. Angry, Bear refuses and gives Matt the big wave board, that he had hidden behind the oil drums on the pier.

The fifth and final act sees the conclusion and resolution of the story. It is known as the 'denouement' and it is here that loose ends from the third and fourth acts are tied up and that character arcs are resolved. Freytag was principally interested in tragedy, so he conceived of this moment as a moment of great catastrophe, though it has since been expanded to allow for the resolution of other kinds of narrative. In *Big Wednesday*, the final act reunites the three friends to brave near-unrideable waves and functions as a coda and a moment of catharsis.

Narrative and Themes

Act 1: The South Swell (Summer 1962)

While the film adopts a fairly traditional structure that, as noted above, has its origins in the theatre, the content of that structure is in many ways impressionistic, particularly in the first act – 'The South

Swell' – which offers a snapshot of youth and the characters' lives when they were in their late teens. In these moments, rather than present a precise and tightly woven narrative, Milius seems to offer a gestural evocation of youth, through sequences that capture discrete moments that build to instil a sense of mythic importance onto the relationships of the friends. While these moments are cumulative and progress the narrative, there is also the sense that any of these sequences could have been swapped out for another – such is the impressionistic quality of the first act. As the film progresses this quality is lessened, with each subsequent act referring back to the first and serving as a marker of the changing relationships among the friends and their relationship with sea, the one constant and an overarching symbol of youth throughout the film. The sea is presented as the domain of youth, while 'moving inland' and 'paying taxes' are seen as part of the inevitability of ageing. The importance of this to the story is most readily communicated through Jack's girlfriend, Sally, who having only recently moved to the area suggests that 'at home being young is just something you do until you grow up. Here, here it's everything'.

The friends divide their time between parties and the beach in a period that is presented as a carefree, youthful idyl. What makes this significantly different from other youth movies is that intergenerational relationships that are typically presented as site of conflict, are not present here, and for the most part parents are absent, with the exception of Jack Barlow's mother, played by William Katt's real life mother, Barbara Hale. She is presented generally as accepting of the antics of her son and his friends, even as they smash up her home, leaving windows and tables broken around them. In these moments, the friends flirt with what it means to be an adult from the relative safety of adolescence. We see parties, brawls, and pranks, tropes common to most teen/youth movies, but there is never any sense of risk, or consequence from these misadventures. These are instead presented as celebratory moments of youthful abandon.

A trip to Mexico functions as the conclusion to Act 1 and, seemingly, appears to be a repetition of the events of the first half of the first act. However, this is simply the first signifier of the end of adolescence and the beginning of adulthood. In Mexico, the narrative continues in much the same vein with a similar emphasis upon parties, brawls, and pranks, but here the events carry with them consequences and repercussions. The shift towards adulthood is evident immediately on their arrival in Tijuana, when Matt's partner Peggy announces that she is pregnant and that she intends to keep the baby. A fight in a strip club later that evening sees Matt knocked to the floor and separated from the rest of the group. Unlike the fights at the earlier party, here there is real risk of harm and we see an attacker pull a knife and stab his assailant. Matt jumps through a window to escape the violence of the bar and finds himself on a street where he sees the body of a sailor lying dead in the gutter, thrown from the balcony above where a prostitute is seen looking down as she smokes a cigarette. As the friends make it back to the car, they find their surf boards missing and the car smashed up. Leroy, evidently married the previous evening, leaves his wife standing by the roadside near a children's playground. As the friends drive off, swings swaying in the breeze seem to signal the end of childhood.

In the final shot of the first act the friends return to the relative safety of their youth, but as Leroy, Matt, and Peggy make their way down the broken steps to the beach, Jack and Sally stay behind, as if separated from their old life by impending adulthood. They walk along to the pier and as they approach its end, they meet Bear, clearly drunk, shouting through the darkness 'Oh, Hell. Move inland, live under a roof, pay taxes, marriage, divorce, the whole damn thing'. He explains that the pier has been condemned and says to Jack, 'you'll be living under the booted foot of the lifeguard state, they've already taken over the point, I won't be able to make your boards anymore. I've got to go and start living like an inlander'.

The first act is most recognisable as that of a traditional youth movie. Here viewers are presented with celebratory images of youth that establish the importance of the place to the people and the friendships that were made at the beach. But, if the primary purpose of the first act is to establish the importance of youth and the relationships that were made there, there is also clear sense that those carefree days are at an end as the first act closes.

Act 2: The West Swell (Fall 1965)

The second act takes place three years after the first and sees Jack, now a lifeguard, patrolling the same beaches he used to surf together with his friends. He opens a letter to find that he has received his draft notification but puts it to one side when he sees a drunken and dishevelled Matt sleeping rough against the beach wall. The friends have already begun to drift apart, with Matt being resentful of Jack's role as lifeguard. However, that gulf grows even further when Matt causes a crash by flailing a ragged blanket in front of a car as if he were a matador. Jack punches him in the face and orders him off the beach, watching until his friend disappears through the broken steps that lead down to the sand.

In the next sequence Matt appears sober and regretful as he walks into Bear's surf shop. In the years since the pier was condemned, surfing has become commercialised, and the Bear is clearly profiting from the upsurge in interest. The shop is lined with the Bear's boards and merchandise and posters of Matt and Jack hang from the ceiling, celebrating them as surfing royalty. Towards the back of the store, the Bear is being fitted for a suit for his upcoming wedding. Matt is sheepish in his approach, head down and uncomfortable, but when Bear sees him he quickly goes to make sure he is okay. Matt explains that he got drunk and caused a wreck and that Jack had hit him but that he was clearly in the wrong. Bear says 'So what? That's when you need a friend, when you're wrong, when you're right you don't need nuthin'. Kids are milling around in background hoping to get a chance to meet their hero, the legendary surfer Matt Johnson and, in a line that seems to predict Jan-Michael Vincent's own downfall (see Chapter 6), Matt says 'I don't want to be a star, I don't want my picture in magazines, I don't want kids looking up to me, I'm a drunk, Bear … a screwup'. Visibly angry, Bear says 'It's just not going right, and you can't understand it. Well growing up's hard, aint it, kid? Those kids do look up to you whether you like it or not'.

Bear reassures Matt, and in the next scene they are together at Bear's wedding, in a sequence that reunites Matt and Jack and stands as yet another marker of the changing priorities of age. Jack arrives with Sally and his mother and is greeted by Bear who passes him a bottle and asks that he drinks with them. Jack explains that he does not drink, but Bear, unwilling to take no for an answer, persists. Jack finally concedes and asks 'What are we drinking to?' Bear replies 'Only to your friends. To your friends, come hell or high water'. The exchange functions as a moment of reconciliation when Jack passes the bottle on to Matt before the friends make their way into the chapel.

The sequence that follows has often been used to justify the inclusion of *Big Wednesday* in lists of notable Vietnam movies, centring as it does on the friends' attempts to dodge the draft. However, while there are serious undertones here, the sequence is presented as a moment of comedic relief with Matt, Waxer, and Leroy respectively feigning a congenital leg injury, homosexuality, and madness. Where the scene does take on a greater significance is in the revelation that Jack voluntarily signed up and is leaving for Vietnam. In the final scene of the second act, the friends are gathered at Jack's home, before he flies out. They are watching news coverage of the Watts riots and Matt comments 'you know, Barlow, you don't need to go all the way to Vietnam, we got a war right here'. It is a sombre moment and as Jack stands to start getting ready to leave, Sally is overcome with emotion and runs out. The friends file past alone or in couples to say farewell to their friend. It is an emotional exchange with the friends variously saying, 'come back to us, Jack', 'don't get your ass shot off', or Leroy's 'you know I'm not the sentimental type but you're going so far away, I really feel funny'. However, it is what Jack says to Matt that resonates the most. The friends embrace as Matt is leaving and Jack looks him squarely in the eyes and says, 'you take care of these people'. Matt looks back, clearly surprised by the level of trust that his friend has placed in him but cautiously agrees.

Michael Ryan and Douglas Kellner's influential work *Camera Politica* argues that this sequence demonstrates the ways in which the friends react negatively to modernity, suggesting that, when faced with footage of urban riots, one of the friends remarks 'people don't know what's good for them' (1990: 225). This line is never uttered; however, they use this in conjunction with the fact that 'the film is shot in a bombastic style that emphasises the primal power of the sea' as evidence that 'its representational surface correlates with the themes of male individuation, the rejection of women, and individual superiority', going on to state that the 'hypertrophic imagery' elevates the 'boys' as 'true fascist "knights"' (1990: 225). It is difficult to know where to begin dismantling such a wilful misinterpretation of both the sequence and the film, suffice to say that the sequence is a poignant moment in the film, and a moment where the mantle of adulthood is passed back to Matt, as Jack goes off to war. This is structurally significant because we do not follow Jack to war and from this point on, it becomes Matt's story.

Act 3: The North Swell (Winter 1968)

The voiceover narration that introduces Act 3 underscores the changes that have taken place in the three years since Act 2, but also since the idyllic days back at the beach in the summer of 1962. The narrator laments the change with the suggestion that 'now it all seemed to be behind us' but that 'the change wasn't in the beach or the rocks or the waves. It was in the people. Some got married. Some moved inland. Some searched for a new spot. Some died'. Cut to Matt standing alone at the rear of the group gathered at the graveside as a military band plays 'The Last Post'. Waxer has died in Vietnam and Matt is seen paying his respects to Waxer's family, telling them that he and Waxer were good friends from the beach. When he meets Peggy at the café afterwards, he's visibly upset and says 'You know of all the friends that Waxer had I was the only one that showed up. It should have meant something'. There is a sense that the friendships that had defined their earlier life were being replaced by family and responsibility, illustrated in Matt's hesitance to get excited at the prospect of moving to a beach front property that Peggy has found. They have received an invite to the premiere of a surfing documentary that features footage of him back in his prime and she convinces him to attend with the suggestion that their daughter, Melissa, would be so proud. They find that footage of him features only peripherally in the documentary and those sequences are not warmly received by the audience who are there to see footage of celebrated surfer Gerry Lopez. For Matt, this encounter only serves to reinforce his belief that, like Waxer, he has been forgotten.

The third act concludes with Jack's return from Vietnam, and his realisation that Sally has moved on and the life he once knew does not exist anymore. The three friends, Matt, Jack and Leroy, are briefly reunited when they meet at the cemetery to pay tribute to their fallen friend and their glory days back at the beach. They get up to leave and embrace, and as they walk between the rows of gravestones a literal divide grows between them. Jack, who has been staying with Matt and Peggy, says 'it's time I move inland, get a job, pay taxes, the whole damn thing'.

Act 4: The Great Swell (Spring 1974)

Act 4 finds Matt, six years on, trying to locate Jack and Leroy at Bear's request. There's a big swell growing, and he hopes to reunite the three to surf at the point together one last time. Matt visits Jack's mother and she suggests that he calls the Ranger's office, where Jack is now working. She asks about Peggy and Melissa, and remembers when the three friends were at Melissa's age, commenting that 'it seems like such a short time to be kids'. Her response inspires an apology from Matt who says, 'I did a lot of things around here I'm kind of ashamed of. I tore up your lawn with my '40 Ford …. Took my pants off in front of your friends … And I even passed out in your closet, but I never, and I don't know who could have if I didn't, but I never, and I repeat never, ever pissed in your steam iron'.

This moment is presented as a moment of levity, in which Hale's Mrs Barlow laughs with Matt, remembering their antics with fondness, a further demonstration, if any were needed, that the intergenerational conflicts common to many youth movies are absent here. It is also presented as a moment of transition for Matt, now the parent, reflecting on the indiscretions of his youth. Matt's paternal role is extended further in the final scene, when he tells a drunken Bear that has been unable to find their friends. Bear, who is now homeless having been divorced and 'drunk up all his money', says 'in all these years there were damn few things that really mattered, but the thing that mattered the most was knowing how you three felt about me, that you respected me and that you felt I'd given you something'. He gestures to Matt and directs him to the big wave board hidden behind the pilings. It is then that Matt tells him 'they're not going to be here tomorrow, Bear. I never gotta a hold of 'em. They're all gone, it's me and you. There's nobody else. It's all gone, there's nothin' left. Let's go home'. When Bear refuses to join him, Matt leaves him on the pier where his old shop used to stand.

Act 5: Big Wednesday (1977)

In the final act, Matt wakes early and makes his way down to the beach to find it swarming with emergency services trying to prevent swimmers and surfers from entering the stormy sea. Undeterred, he descends the broken steps to find his friends waiting for him at the bottom, as if they had never left. They smile and begin their walk to the shoreline, set against a swelling militaristic theme. The sequence has audio and visual echoes of the conclusion to Sam Peckinpah's New Hollywood classic, *The Wild Bunch* (1969), only here the warriors are surfers engaged in a pitched battle with the sea (see Figure 2.1).

Figure 2.1 In crafting the conclusion to *Big Wednesday* Milius invokes the climactic scene of Sam Peckinpah's *The Wild Bunch* (1969)

Trumpets sound a fanfare as each of the friends, Matt, Jack, and Leroy, is called to go down to the sea to surf, 'a swell so big and so strong it'll wipe clean everything that came before it'. It is into this arena that the friends step, each taking turns as celebrated surfer Gerry Lopez looks on, a validation, if any were needed, that they were as good as everyone had always said they were.

The waves continue to grow and Matt, the last of the three to surf, is wiped-out by a 20-foot pipeline and dragged to the bottom of the sea. Jack and Leroy manage to rescue their struggling friend who limps out of the water and across the beach. As they are leaving the beach, a kid hands Matt his board and says 'that was the hottest ride I've ever seen'. Matt looks up at the big wave board, pausing and, in a moment that seems to function as an acknowledgement that this is the best he is ever going to be, he passes the board back to the kid and says, 'keep it, and if it ever gets big again you can go out and ride it'. Another kid on the clifftop asks Bear if he is a surfer, to which he replies, 'not me, I'm a garbageman', so impressed is he by the three friends and the way that they distinguished themselves. The friends climb back through the broken hoardings barring the entryway to the beach and vow to keep in touch.

The narrative has an incredible sense of economy, facilitated in part by the five-act structure and a timeline that spans a fifteen-year period. While this could easily have collapsed in on itself, it is held together by the voice of the narrator who guides the audience through the seasons of the film. Milius has stated on a number of occasions that as a writer he was inspired by the great American writers: Jack Kerouac, John Steinbeck, and Herman Melville, and that influence can certainly be seen all over *Big Wednesday*, but particularly in the film's narration. Much like Kerouac's autobiographical character Sal Paradise in *On the Road* (1957), Ishmael, the only surviving crew member of the *Pequod* and narrator of Melville's *Moby Dick* (1851), and the unnamed omniscient observer who guides the reader through Steinbeck's *The Grapes of Wrath* (1939), *Big Wednesday*'s narrator (played by actor Robert Englund), is the well-placed observer who returns at the beginning of every act, to reflect on the ways the friends' lives had changed in the intervening years.

Milius has said that he always imagined *Big Wednesday* as a coming-of-age story with Arthurian overtones, and nowhere are those allusions to myth more evident than in the interactions with the Bear. His narrative is a secondary thread that runs through the story and infuses it with a mythic quality. Bear is introduced through the narrator who says, 'Bear made our boards and told us stories. He knew where the waves came from and why. Like the surfers that came before us, we saw everything in the Bear'. When the audience is first introduced to Bear he is building a big wave board, describing when and where it would be used to two young surfers who tell him how much they admire the surfing of Matt, Jack, and Leroy. Bear says that while they are good, they need more experience and that they could get it too, if they would only keep on surfing. The kids are puzzled by Bear's response, saying 'what do you mean, those guys will surf forever?' to which Bear replies 'nobody surfs forever', the first sense the audience gets that the carefree days spent at the beach surfing might not last forever.

This brief moment of foreshadowing comes immediately before another in which Bear hints towards the dramatic conclusion to the film, in an exchange between him, the kids, and the character actor Hank Worden, who plays the character 'Shopping Cart' in the film and who featured in many of John Ford's films, including *The Searchers* (1956). Describing when the big wave board would be ridden, the Bear says:

> It would take a big day. But then you hear talk of a big day every now and then. It'll happen again. It happened in '50. It'll be a swell so big and strong it'll wipe clean everything that came before it. That's when this board will be ridden, and that is when Matt, Jack and Leroy, they can distinguish themselves, that's the day they can draw the line.

In the director's commentary for *Big Wednesday*, Milius refers to the big wave board explicitly as 'Excalibur', a confirmation, if any were needed, of the mythic scale of the ideas that underpin *Big Wednesday*. The commentary gives a clear insight into the ways in which Milius was incorporating those Arthurian overtones into the narrative. In their exploration of the connections between ancient myths and contemporary culture, Amy T. Peterson and David J. Dunworth argue that Excalibur, while widely known, is also one of the most misunderstood symbols in all mythology. They argue that, all too often, Excalibur is simply accepted as the weapon of the hero, citing Beowolf and his Hrunting, Luke Skywalker and his lightsaber and, even Dirty Harry Callaghan and his .45 Magnum (2004: 52). Instead, they argue that Excalibur has 'transcended the simple description of a gilded long sword and become a symbol of the strength, pride, and power of an age long passed, yet attainable once again' (2004: 52). Conceiving of the big wave board as Excalibur makes the passing of the board at the end of the film all the more poignant; Matt is passing a symbol of strength, pride, and power, the longboard from an age long since passed, onto the next generation. Elsewhere, Milius has stated that:

> The story of *Big Wednesday* is a myth, but it's really like a piece of medieval poetry. Most of your epic medieval poetry is the story of friendship tested against a force of the supernatural. In *Moby Dick* there is the supernatural; there's Moby Dick, more than a whale, more than a quest. In this case it's the 'big day', the testing, when the gods test the men to see if they are worthy.
>
> (quoted in MacGillivray 1978a: 608)

Within this mythic framework, Bear is clearly the mentor, a long-established archetype in narratives that draw upon classical mythology, and a trope famously employed by George Lucas with Obe-Wan Kenobe in the *Star Wars* universe. Lucas built his narrative around Joseph Campbell's seminal *The Hero with a Thousand Faces* (2012), a book of comparative mythology first published in 1949 in which Campbell argued that the mythologies of the world shared common tropes and conventions and could be reduced to a single 'monomyth' (Campbell 2012: 1). Lucas used this as a template to construct a vast cinematic universe that has been celebrated as much as it has been denigrated and become the basis for much of the world building in contemporary franchised entertainment. Despite their friendship, when asked about the importance of myth, Milius said:

> People talk about it all the time [...] you know George Lucas talks about it all the time. He doesn't know how to use it at all. He doesn't understand myth at all. As illustrated by [*The*] *Phantom Menace*. Writers who really understand myth don't use it consciously. There are very few things that are truly mythical. There's a lot of stuff that's famous, but very few things that are the stuff of myth and legend.
>
> (quoted in Bauer 2015)

Irrespective of one's views on the *Star Wars* universe, myth is layered into *Big Wednesday* and implicitly delivered, as opposed to the overt and explicit textual role that it plays in the *Star Wars* universe. In *Big Wednesday* myth imbues what is otherwise an overtly sentimental male melodrama with a sense of scale and importance, and while it is likely this that people are responding to with claims that the film is grandiose and pretentious, it undeniably elevates the ambitions of the film. Milius has said that 'There was a lot of pressure to make it more like *Animal House*', but argues that 'the movie has a huge following now because it did have loftier ambitions. It was not just a story about somebody trying to ride the biggest wave or something. That's not enough' (quoted in Bauer 2015). While the point stands, *National Lampoon's Animal House* (Landis, 1978), wasn't released until after *Big Wednesday* and was the property of another studio, so where exactly the pressure to alter *Big Wednesday* was coming from is not clear.

Style and Aesthetics

Stephen Prince suggests that as a director, Milius 'is classically inclined' and that 'the editing in his films usually respects spatial continuity while the camera work is unobtrusive and does not draw attention to itself avoiding the use of zoom and complex camera movements (Prince, quoted in Leotta 2018: 15). This perspective is mirrored in Milius' own account and his suggestion that he 'like(s) to represent scenes as the eyes would see them – with no gimmicky camera tricks [...] straightforward photography with strong cross or backlight to shape and texture everything well (MacGillivray, 1978a: 572). This emphasis on functional simplicity suggests a restrained director, certainly a director who is more invested in progressing the story, than perhaps in the artistry with which it is delivered – an idea that sits counter to what is widely believed about Milius and his reputation for excess. Indeed, while his films are characterised by a preoccupation with violence, they are rarely gruesome in their representation of sadistic or violent acts and these elements are only ever presented in the service of the story (Prince, quoted in Leotta 2018: 15). This classical inclination draws comparisons with directors like John Huston, a director with whom Milius collaborated twice and held in great esteem. Huston, like Milius, wrote the screenplays for most of the feature films he directed. However, unlike Milius, largely because of the period in which he was working, but also because of a perceived absence of directorial style, Huston was never considered an auteur, rather an adapter of his own work. As Bruce Jackson has argued, 'there is no Huston visual or even narrative style; nothing on the screen marks him as auteur' (Jackson 2019). Milius might be discussed in similar terms; however, while he demonstrates a similar economy in his directorial approach, there are still stylistic qualities that are present in much of his work that mark them out as uniquely his. For instance, Alfio Leotta highlights his predilection for voiceover narration and suggests that this 'sets the nostalgic tone of [his] films' and frames his stories as mythic tales. Leotta observes that this technique is often 'complemented by a montage of period photos and

Figure 2.2 Frames as thresholds: sub-framing in *Big Wednesday* as an homage to John Ford's *The Searchers* (1956)

SURFERS
RULE

newspaper clippings which clearly position the story is a specific historical moment' (2018: 15), a technique used to great effect in the opening credits of *Big Wednesday.*

Nostalgia is mobilised in a number of different ways in *Big Wednesday.* However, one of the most intriguing borrows heavily from another 'classical' Hollywood director, and another notable influence of Milius – John Ford. Ford's epic western *The Searchers* (1956) begins with Dorothy Jordan's Martha, silhouetted against the subframe of a doorway leading out to the expansive mesas, cliffs, and buttes of Monument Valley. Richard Hutson has argued that in this initial framing 'the human drama seems too close to the buttes and the desert. The valley encroaches upon the human activity – or rather, human enterprise has extended too far into a land that cannot support it' (2004: 93). It is a similar sensibility that informs the introduction to *Big Wednesday.* The broken fence that frames the crumbling steps and the wilderness of the ocean beyond evokes the sense of a lost culture, and of human enterprise that has similarly extended too far, only here, the ocean has reclaimed the contested land. Milius' demonstrable commitment to mythic narratives encourages a reading of Matt, Jack, and Leroy as the last surviving heroes of a long-forgotten culture, with the broken-down façade representing the fading remnants of that culture (see Figure 2.2). Much like the omniscient voice of the narrator, this sub-framing can be understood as a device through which Milius nostalgically recalls his own youth, a wistful representation of memory, framed through broken pillars.

In an assessment of nostalgia in film, Pam Cook explores the use of screens, mirrors, windows, and extremely tight framing in Wong Kar-Wai's *In the Mood for Love* (2000), suggesting that 'it is as though history is being viewed through the filter of nostalgic memory […] to imply a perspective coloured by distance and obstructed vision' (2005: 9). While Milius' use of sub-framing in *Big Wednesday* is a clear nod to Ford and *The Searchers,* there is also a sense that, as with Wong Kar-Wai, this is a history viewed through the filter of nostalgic memory, a captured moment that only exists within the frame. Frames as thresholds feature prominently throughout *Big Wednesday,* not just in the framing of the entrance to the beach but also in Leroy's psychological evaluation at the draft board, another instance in which the sub-frame suggests a threshold being crossed.

This metaphor can be pushed further, and Bear's wedding can be seen as a continuation of this theme viewed through the symbolism of Ford. As Michael Budd has noted, 'in the Westerns of Ford, civilisation is embodied primarily by the family and the community' (1976: 62), with the wedding itself a recurring motif and important symbol of civilisation. Arguably,

Bear's wedding serves a similar purpose in *Big Wednesday*, as both a symbol of civilisation in its commitment to family and community, and in the suggestion of a move away from the wilderness, a wilderness that in Ford is typified in the mesas, cliffs, and buttes of Monument Valley, and in *Big Wednesday* by the frontier wilderness of the North Pacific Ocean. All of these elements add to the mythic quality of the film, and they all illustrate the debt that the film owes to 'classical' Hollywood and the continuities between Milius and his forebears. In style-oriented accounts, New Hollywood is often presented as a break from the conventions of the 'classical' Hollywood system and suggests the emergence of a more fragmented 'post-classical' style which broke with the traditions of the 'classical' Hollywood period (King 2002: 3). However, what we see with Milius is a continuation of the approaches and practices that had defined the earlier period.

It is impossible to discuss the style and aesthetics of *Big Wednesday* without offering some discussion of the technical challenges faced in the realisation of the film, of which there were many. Hollywood's rendering of surfing had always suffered from a lack of realism, with producers invariably opting for rear-projection rather than face the technical difficulties of actually getting in the water and filming. Even Bruce Brown's celebrated surf documentary, *Endless Summer* (1966), had failed to fully wrestle with the issue of how to capture the energy of surfing and was reduced to capturing the action from a distance on 16mm film from the shoreline. Milius knew he needed something more dynamic, so he approached Greg MacGillivray, who, with his partner Jim Freeman, had produced a number of surfing films that had begun to narrow the gap between the experience of surfing and its cinematic representation. MacGillivray filmed from boats and developed specialist water-proof camera rigs that he mounted to surfboards, enabling him to get in the water with the surfers and capture the action close-up. By the time Milius was shooting *Big Wednesday*, the MacGillivray Freeman company had firmly established a reputation for being able to capture the excitement of adventure sports. Like Milius, MacGillivray was also a surfer, so it was important to him that the sequences come close to capturing the reality of surfing. When interviewed many years later, MacGillivray would say that it is 'very difficult to convey to people the beauty and feeling of surfing. It's something that's very difficult to talk about, let alone write a script about', and he conceded that he did not believe that any film had managed to fully capture that experience, including *Big Wednesday*, though he did believe that the film came closer than most: 'explaining that feeling is such an elusive thing' (MacGillivray, quoted in Loose 2009).

Attempting to capture the elusive qualities of surfing would push the team to devise innovative audio and visual solutions to address the range of technical problems that they were facing. The team developed eleven distinct waterproof housings and cameras that were each designed, built, and tested with a different purpose in mind. Eight of the eleven were extremely compact, designed to be portable in the impact zone with each using specific lenses and running at specific frame rates, while the other three were larger and therefore capable of housing longer lenses and carrying heavier 4000-front-load film magazines. Gregg MacGillivray explained:

> To further intensify the action and excitement of the big wave sequences, they photographed close, sometimes with as many as three cameramen positioned right beneath the breaking wave. This angle, looking up at the wave with the wide angled lens, magnified the inherent power of the wave, making it enormous. To increase the size of the wave even further, [they] used an unorthodox framing style. Taking advantage of the Panavision wide-screen frame, which is relatively short in height, we cropped off the top of the wave, giving the audience the feeling of an unlimited height to the wave, extending far above the top of the screen to the roof of the theatre. In this manner, we were able to make 20-foot waves look 40 feet in height.
>
> (MacGillivray 1978b: 580)

While these visual elements were pivotal in the realisation of the film, capturing the dialogue amongst the 20-foot waves proved no less challenging. The actors would be placed amongst suitably dramatic waves far out of the reach of the soundman's boat, so the team designed waterproof wireless microphones that were embedded into each of the actor's surfboards. They would then position the actors and wait for a set of big waves. MacGillivray details that:

> Once the set began, we had only seconds to complete the scene. Hurriedly, the soundman on shore would signal that his sound was 'rolling'. John Milius who was sitting on another surfboard behind me, would then yell, 'Action!' and the actors would complete their lines while hopefully not drifting out of position. Even with perfect performances by the actors, we often had to shoot at least ten takes to get the correct positions for the sun, surfers and waves.
>
> (MacGillivray 1978b: 611–12)

Despite the various challenges, the combined effect of the audio-visual elements helped to create an aesthetic that is still celebrated as a high watermark in how filmmakers approach filming surfing today.

Conclusion

Ideas of youth and what it means to be young are central to the success of *Big Wednesday*. From its opening narration to its closing theme, the film is a lamentation of lost youth and a celebration of friendship. Presented in a series of almost interchangeable vignettes, the film has an impressionistic quality that effectively captures a sense of the beach as a carefree coastal idyl far removed from the realities of impending adulthood. The challenges faced by the friends mark their transition from youth to young adulthood, while the sea serves as a constant reminder of what has been lost. This creates a sense of the ocean as frontier, that borrows heavily from western directors, especially John Ford and Sam Peckinpah, and that works to imbue the film with a mythic sensibility that was always central to Milius' ambitions for the film. Described as 'a coming-of-age story with Arthurian overtones', the structure and plot differ greatly from the approaches generally favoured by Hollywood during this period and help to give the film a dramatic sensibility that borrows heavily from theatrical and operatic presentations, and this again gives the film a sense of mythic importance that has surely contributed to its longevity.

Note

1 Between 1959 and 1970, Severson would make a number of short surf films. *Big Wednesday*, released in 1961, is perhaps his most celebrated.

3 Resistance and Incorporation in Californian Surf Culture

Alongside the cowboy, the surfer is one of the most enduring images of American popular culture. It is an image that has been remediated across film, music, fashion, and journalism, and is so established in the popular imagination that it borders on sociological cliché. The blonde-haired, blue-eyed, unintelligent but affable beach bum, part-stoner, part-spiritual guru has become a dominant cultural stereotype. The image was popularised by Sean Penn's performance as Jeff Spicoli in *Fast Times at Ridgemont High* (Heckerling, 1982), and distilled into the sea turtle Crush, in Disney/Pixar's *Finding Nemo* (Stanton, 2003), a film that presents an animated character with all the vocal and gestural characteristics of a 'surfer dude'. It is an image that carries with it a countercultural sensibility, the radical hedonist who has opted out of society, but also one that was formed in the wake of the commercialisation and commodification of surfing as the number one Southern Californian pastime. The sport grew out of an initially small subculture to be popularised by the beach party movies and the surf rock sound of the late 1950s and early 1960s.

The culture industries have long presented the sun-kissed shores of Southern California as carefree youthful idyl, far removed from the melodramatic tales of inner city troubled youth that had come to dominate youth cinema of the 1950s. Surfing was presented as a clean-cut antidote to films that dramatised social ills, and while surfers were often considered juvenile delinquents in their own communities (see Irwin [1962]), popular culture created a publicly acceptable image that smoothed over the rough edges and rehabilitated the Californian surfer into a wholesome brand that could be exported worldwide. Those who had been part of the grass-roots community and who had practised surfing long before Hollywood became interested, were understandably aggrieved and did not recognise themselves in the saccharine images that came to dominate the media landscape. Some offered alternative images

DOI: 10.4324/9780429058295-4

that they felt better represented their subculture, only for these alternatives to be incorporated into the dominant image of the surfer and surfing. The resultant image is a complex amalgam that is the product of waves of commodification, resistance, and incorporation that dates back to turn-of-the-century Hawai'i.

This chapter will explore these tensions through a consideration of three key moments in the commercialisation of the sport. Beginning with the surfing boom of the 1960s, this chapter will first examine what happened when Hollywood became interested in surfing in the late 1950s and early 1960s, with a view to understanding how this affected the grass-roots surfing communities who failed to recognise themselves in the remediated images of Californian surf culture. Second, it will historicise efforts to commercialise surfing, through a review of the promotional strategy implemented by The Hawai'i Promotion Committee (HPC) at the turn of the twentieth century, an organisation that sold the benefits of surfing as part of a broader tourism strategy. Finally, the chapter will conclude with an exploration of the legitimatisation of the sport, from the lobbying that resulted in corporate sponsorship, to the sport debuting at the 2020 Summer Olympics in Tokyo, Japan. These three points provide a valuable insight into the processes of commodification that have helped to shape the popular image of surfing over the course of the twentieth century, but also a context to understand how the community of surfers desperately tried to resist the commodification of their subculture – a narrative mirrored by *Big Wednesday*.

The Commodification of Youth Culture

In her book *Golden State, Golden Youth*, Kirse Granat May explains that the baby boom generation grew up in a mass media environment dominated by images of California (May 2002: 95). These images both capitalised on and commodified Californian adolescence though popular music, television, and film, the success of which she attributes to broader cultural shifts that were taking place in the United States and that were attempting 'to resolve by denial the problems that emerged in the sixties with a more satisfying and less threatening picture of its youth' (2). While May highlights the 1960s as the beginning of perceived problems around America's youth, these issues actually emerged in the 1950s, and a decade that was marked by a pre-occupation with juvenile delinquency. In his exploration of what he calls the 'cycle of outrage', James Gilbert observes a sharp rise in the perception of juvenile delinquency between 1953 and 1958 (1988: 64). Gilbert argues that while the Children's Bureau and the Attorney General's Committee may have first alerted the public to the problem that the juvenile delinquent posed, the threat was amplified in the media, in radio and television specials, newsreels, feature films, magazines, and newspapers, all of which presented 'delinquency as if it were something altogether new in this period in American history' (63). In film, this preoccupation is typically seen to culminate in *Rebel without a Cause* (Ray, 1955) and *Blackboard Jungle* (Brooks, 1955), inspired by the success of *The Wild One* in the previous year (Benedek, 1954). The success of these films would stimulate a cycle of teen films that would continue into the 1960s, and while few would achieve the success of *Rebel without a Cause* and *Blackboard Jungle,* the films did contribute to the formation of a discrete genre – the teenpic.

Thomas Doherty attributes the emergence of the teenpic to the decline of classical Hollywood cinema and the arrival of the teenager as a distinct and potentially profitable consumer (2002: 12). This is a perspective mirrored in Jon Savage's account in which he suggests that 'for the first time, youth had become its own target market [...] it had become a discrete age group with its own rituals, right and demands' (2007: xxi). Despite an acknowledgment of the existence of the genre, Savage is cynical of its application, arguing that the designation of the teenager 'from the very start, was a marketing term used by advertisers and manufactures that reflected the newly visible spending power of adolescents' (2007: xxi). Hollywood quickly recognised the profitability of the teenage market and was only too keen to capitalise on the success of the youth movement, adapting its output by creating cycles of film that appealed squarely to this new demographic. Doherty offers a detailed case study of the evolution of the teenpic, charting its emergence with the juvenile delinquent movie, and its development through its successors, the rock 'n' roll movie, the horror movie and the 'clean' teenpic, presenting each as distinct cycles in the evolution of the teen movie. For Doherty, 'clean teenpics featured an aggressively normal, traditionally good-looking crew of fresh young faces, "good kids" who preferred dates to drugs and crushes to crime. Sweet, sanitised, and sun-drenched, they gave a bright but bowdlerised update to familiar romantic-comedic situations' (2002: 159). So successful were these films that Catherine Driscoll has argued that 'in the heyday of the Production Code there were delinquents and there were clean teens and little in between' (2011: 20).

This is important because the film that popularised and commodified surf culture is considered as a typical example of the clean teen movie cycle and is often presented as a conservative reaction to the cycle of juvenile delinquency films detailed above (see May 2002: 67, Doherty 2002: 160–1). *Gidget* (Wendkos, 1959) was an adaptation of the novel *Gidget: The Little Girl with Big Ideas* (1957) written by the screenwriter Frederick Kohner about his daughter Kathy's adventures surfing at Malibu. The cultural impact of the film was unprecedented, becoming what Matt Warshaw has called 'the starting bell for a nine-year surf boom that took the sport from a Californian centric phenomenon to a national craze to a hot international export' (2010: 156). However, while many are keen to attribute the widespread cultural appeal and adoption of surfing to *Gidget* alone, Warshaw cautions against such an approach, suggesting that *Gidget* was simply one part of a broader appeal to teenage consumerism that saw:

> Tens of thousands of people slow danced to 'Surfer Girl' and thronged to the local Bijou to see *Ride the Wild Surf*; they shopped at May Company and bought nylon competition strip trunks from the McGregor surfing collection, Hang-Ten sneakers, and Cute ex 'Wipe Out Pink' toenail polish. Coppertone and Jantzen rolled out surf themed ad campaigns – no surprise there. A ubiquitous Hamm's beer billboard showed Rusty Miller jamming down the face at Sunset Beach. Pepsi did surf ads. So did Triumph, Mobile, Chevy and Dewar's […]. As *The Saturday Evening Post* put it in 1967, surfing was 'the most successful California export since the orange'.
>
> (Warshaw 2010: 187)

So attractive was this image of Californian youth culture that according to Mike Purpus, even landlocked 'people in Kentucky and Kansas and Tennessee […] were buying surfboards just to put 'em on top of their cars and drive around so they could pick up chicks' (quoted in Moore 2010: 28–9). *Gidget* would become the inaugural entry in a transmedia franchise that would last for almost 30 years and provided the template on which other studios would capitalise, most notably American International Pictures (AIP), through its 'Beach Party' series of movies with Frankie Avalon and Annette Funicello. Surf music would provide the soundtrack to the boom, initially through the aggressive instrumental stylings of Dick Dale & His Del-Tones, and then later through the softer vocal harmonies of Jan and Dean and The Beach Boys. Surfers developed their own vocabulary, their own gestures, and their own fashions and, in the summer of 1960, *The Surfer*, the first magazine devoted to surfing appeared. It was followed in quick succession by *Surfing Illustrated* (1962), *The Surf Guide*

(1963), and *Petersen's Surfing Magazine* (1963). Through this exposure surfing grew exponentially, from an estimated 10,000 American surfers in the pre-*Gidget* 1950s to conservative estimates of 200,000 and wildly exaggerated estimates of several million by 1965 (Warshaw 2010: 201).

In his work on the surf film Douglas Booth argues that for America's youth 'surfing symbolised carefree fun in a period of economic prosperity and political idealism' (1996: 313). This perspective is shared by Kirse Granat May in her assessment of *Gidget* as an 'idealised portrayal of teenage life in California' that 'highlighted the wholesomeness' of youth and that presented Gidget as 'a heroine marked by conformity' that offered a move away from the brooding male archetype established by James Dean in *Rebel without a Cause* (May 2002: 67–8, 76). This same emphasis on conformity can been seen in AIP's Beach Party cycle of movies, which Gary Morris suggests 'show teenagers as wistful, comic, conformist creatures, sexless and predictable, ultimately willing to carry on the traditions of consumer capitalism that they, as voracious consumers themselves, clearly benefit from' (1993: 4). However, while Booth and May are keen to embrace Gidget as a symbol of conformity, Pamela Robertson Wojcik rejects their ideas, arguing that 'critics [who] read Gidget as non-rebellious' are 'reading the mainstreaming of surfing not as caused by Gidget but as proof of her conformity' (2021: 34–5). This is an important distinction, because it recognises the fluidity of the image of the surfer throughout this period, and the rehabilitation of a group who were largely considered deviants prior to the surfing boom. Sociologist John Keith Irwin claims that surfers' 'parties became notorious for their abandon. Extreme drunkenness, sexual promiscuity, fighting, and physical damage to the houses were the marks of a good surfing party' (1973: 153). Public exhibitionism and lewd behaviour were commonplace, even daubing swastikas on their surf boards, parading around in Nazi uniforms, and performing Nazi salutes (see Figure 3.1). This is an image far removed from the saccharine representations facilitated by *Gidget*.

Waves of Resistance and Incorporation

Michael Scott Moore suggests that 'it's possible that no other American subculture has moved from wildness and authenticity to Technicolor cheese as quickly as the [surfing] scene in Malibu' (2010: 28). The mainstreaming of surfing left many in the grass-roots communities concerned, but as Krista Comer observes, while 'the Gidget phenomenon generated subcultural foreboding about the potential costs to surf culture of its newfound popularity, it also generated a host of creative and financial possibilities' (2004: 238). An industry emerged overnight and for those

Figure 3.1 A subculture within a subculture: white youths perform Nazi salutes while heading to the beach in California to surf, 1961 (screengrab from *Waves Apart* [2022])

who were already steeped in the subculture, there were newfound opportunities to capitalise on its success. Though admittedly, for many, this was often only to counter the glossy image projected by Hollywood and the culture industries. Renowned surfer John Severson (director of the original *Big Wednesday*, see Chapter 2), created *Surfer* magazine expressly for those reasons, later saying, 'surfers hated those Hollywood surf films, and I could see that *Surfer* could create a truer image of the sport' (quoted in Howe 2017).

It is arguably this same impulse that drove Milius to make *Big Wednesday*, a film considered by many to be the 'anti-Gidget', an antidote to the beach party movies of the 1960s, and a Hollywood blockbuster that would finally give the sport of surfing some legitimacy (Kaser 2013). Of course, that would not happen, at least not initially. Significantly, one of the many criticisms levelled at *Big Wednesday* by Janet Maslin in her 1978 review was that while the score incorporated a number of hit songs from the early 1960s, the absence of 'surf music' was a significant oversight. Maslin argued that 'surely The Beach Boys or Jan and Dean were just as deeply in love with the sport as Mr. Milius, and for them, too, it had connotations of masculine daring' (Maslin 1978: C14). What Maslin failed to recognise were the tensions that had long existed in the surfing community and the desire to capture an *authentic* representation of the lifestyle free of the baggage of commerce and commodification.

The tensions born out of the resistance are common threads and are expressed in the narratives of individual surfers who lived through the boom years. However, they can also be seen in the narratives of scholars and cultural commentators, many of whom were similarly keen to separate the industry out into an organic, and therefore authentic, industry, and a commodified, and therefore inauthentic, industry. Mark Stranger argues that 'while surfing culture was being appropriated for popular consumption the subculture was developing independently in a more subversive direction through its own magazines, its own movies and an affinity with the co-emergent counterculture movement' (2011: 189). Douglas Booth similarly attempts to separate the culture, identifying three distinct genres of surf movie: 'Hollywood "beach stories"', 'aficionado "Pure" surfing films', and 'surfing industry films' (1996: 313). Booth suggests that 'Pure' surfing films 'focused on wave locations, board designs, riding styles, and cultural trends' and were a continuation of a kind of filmmaking that had begun in the 1930s with the home movies of early Californian surfers Doc Ball, John Larronde, and Don James, a genre of film that can be seen to culminate with Bruce Brown's cult classic *The Endless Summer* (1966).

These were films produced by surfers for surfers and documented their own lives at the beach and the pleasure that they took in riding waves. Because of that, they are often imagined as removed from the capitalistic drive that would underpin much of surf culture of the 1960s. However, while Stranger is keen to conceive of these as separate industries that operate independently of each other, there is a convergence that is impossible to deny, and therefore ultimately, separate. *The Endless Summer* is widely regarded as the definitive surf movie and, because it is film 'made by surfers for a limited surfing audience and typically exhibited at surf clubs' (Ormrod 2005a: 39), it is considered by many to sit outside of the capitalistic drive that underpins Hollywood's flirtation with the surf movie. However, Joan Ormrod also argues that it is 'impossible to wrest the film from its consumerist roots' (2005a: 40). This mirrors the writing of Dick Hebdige who, in relation to subcultures, has argued:

> As soon as the original innovations which signify 'subculture' are translated into commodities and made generally available, they become 'frozen'. Once removed from their private contexts by the

> small entrepreneurs and big fashion interests who produce them on a mass scale, they become codified, made comprehensible, rendered at once public property and profitable merchandise. In this way, the two forms of incorporation (the semantic/ideological and the 'real' commercial) can be said to converge on the commodity form.
>
> (Hebdige 1979: 96)

While Stranger and Booth are both keen to maintain a separation between the ideological and the commercial interests at work here, there is an inevitable blurring that happens in the commodification of youth culture. Though, for the purposes of this volume, rather than think of these as fixed points of convergence, it is perhaps more useful to conceive of these as waves of commodification and resistance, in which the subculture is appropriated by the mainstream, and then various interventions are made by the subculture to retain ownership. While these interventions initially function as sites of resistance, they are gradually also subsumed and incorporated into the dominant image of the culture.

Because of the countercultural connotations of surfing, particularly during this period, it is useful to frame this discussion through a broader understanding of counterculture and how its imagery and iconography are gradually subsumed into mainstream capitalistic process. In his exploration of 1960s West Coast rock, John Storey explains that this was 'a music which had developed from the 'bottom' up, and not a music imposed from the 'top' down. But like all popular cultural initiatives under capitalism, it faced three possible futures: marginalisation, disappearance, or incorporation into the system's profit-making concerns', concluding that 'countercultural rock's future was incorporation' (2009: 92). The same is true of surfing. Countercultural activity often imagines itself as existing outside of these processes but, and as Thomas Frank has argued, the 'commercial fantasies of rebellion, liberation and outright "revolution" against the stultifying demands of mass society are commonplace and almost to the point of invisibility in advertising, movies, and television programming' (1997: 4). In what reads as a damning commentary on popular culture, Frank enumerates that:

> Nike shoes are sold to the accompaniment of words delivered by William S. Burroughs and songs by The Beatles, Iggy Pop, and Gil Scott Heron ('the revolution will not be televised'); peace symbols decorate a line of cigarettes manufactured by R.J. Reynolds and the walls and windows of Starbucks coffee shops nationwide; the

> products of Apple, IBM, and Microsoft are touted as devices of liberation; and advertising across the product-category spectrum calls upon consumers to break rules and find themselves [...] A host of self-designated 'corporate-revolutionaries' [...] gravitate naturally to the imagery of rebel youth culture to dramatize their own insurgent vision.
>
> (Frank 1997: 4–5)

Why would surfing be any different? And while Booth and Stranger are keen to present a bifurcated industry in which authentic surfers resisted the incorporation of their lifestyle into the system's profit-making concerns, in reality, their resistance simply augmented the popular image of surfing and helped to underscore the countercultural tendency that would become such an integral part of the dominant image of the Californian surfer. What is perhaps most interesting here, is that despite opposition from the surfing community, this was not the first attempt to commodify and commercialise the sport. Indeed, the surfing subculture would not have existed in Southern California at all, were it not for previous attempts to commodify and therefore profit from the sport.

Historicising the Commodification of Surfing

The history of surfing, and therefore the history of the commodification of surfing, is irrevocably tied to colonisation and the expansion of empire under both British and North American rule. And while the practice of surfing is believed to date back as far as three or four thousand years in Polynesia, Micronesia, and the Hawai'ian Islands (O'Brian 1995: 83; Scures 1986: 4), the earliest known written account of surfing comes from the journals of Captain Cook and an entry made by the ship's surgeon, Dr William Anderson. In 1777, while Cook was moored at Matavai Bay, Tahiti, Anderson's diary captures with fascination one particularly adept wave rider, observing that:

> He went out far from the shore, till he was near the place where the swell begins to rise; and, watching its first motion very attentively, paddled before it, with great quickness, till he found that it overtook him, and had acquired sufficient force to carry his canoe before it, without passing underneath. He then sat motionless and was carried along, at the same swift rate as the wave, till it landed him upon the beach. I could not help concluding that this man felt the most supreme pleasure while he was driven on so fast and so smoothly by the sea; especially as, though the tents and ships were

> so near, he did not seem in the least, to envy, or even to take any notice of, the crowds of his countrymen collected to view them as objects which were rare and curious.
>
> (Cook 1784: 150)

Despite winning Anderson's admiration, Cook's arrival would spread terror across the islands, seeing him torch entire villages and carve crosses into the natives' flesh (Subin 2022: 366). The culture of Hawai'i's remote archipelago was almost destroyed through exposure to European disease and alcohol. This cultural decline continued throughout the nineteenth century when Calvinist missionaries imposed conservative Christian beliefs, political systems, and consumer values on the natives. Drew Kampion and Bruce Brown argue that 'surfing's association with nakedness, sexuality, wagering, shameless exuberance, informality, ignorant joy and freedom were counter-productive to the designs of the church fathers', and that surfing itself was almost lost in the expansion of empire (1998: 33).

Most contemporary accounts of the history of surfing reiterate this perspective and suggest that it was through these combined forces that the sport was driven to the brink of extinction. Most also erroneously claim that the sport would have died out completely were it not for the actions of one Alexander Hume Ford, a former writer, magazine editor, playwright, and photographer, who had relocated to Honolulu in 1907 and quickly became fascinated with surfing. While Ford would become a great publicist and promoter of the sport, surfing had already been identified as key to repositioning Hawai'i as a profitable tourist resort in a global marketplace. This was a critical juncture in Hawai'ian history, and as Scott Laderman has detailed, 'following Hawaii's annexation by the United States in 1898, a number of Americans sought to profit from the islands' tropical climate by further opening up the territory to tourists as what one promotional booklet called "a marvellous out-of-door wonderland, a picnic ground from the earth"' (2014: 17).

The Hawaii Promotion Committee (HPC) was key to this strategy. Established in February of 1903 following conversations between Honolulu's Chamber of Commerce and the Merchants' Association, the HPC was formed to 'advertise the attractions of the Territory of Hawaii, promote tourist travel, disseminate literature and, by correspondence with tourist agencies, steamship and railroad companies' to 'enlist their aid and assistance in directing travellers and tourists to the Territory' ('By-Laws of the Chamber of Commerce', quoted in Mak 2015: 25). Patrick Moser suggests that the initial goals of the organisation were to induce East Coast professionals to emigrate to the islands, but when that proved fruitless, Harry P. Wood took over as secretary and in 1905 shifted the focus of the organisation's strategy towards tourism, specifically targeting visitors from North America's West Coast (Moser 2020: 505). Wood, a Hawai'ian national who had spent over 15 years in San Diego, highlighted surfing as one of the key Hawai'ian traditions that would help to stimulate the growth of the economy and help Hawai'i brand itself in a global marketplace, and therefore began developing strategies with key stakeholders in California. In 1906, 129 years after Anderson's encounter and under Wood's direction, the HPC commissioned Thomas Edison's studio to produce what would be the first footage of surfing ever captured on film. Comprised of over 30 scenes that take place over three sequences and that collectively last for more than 42 minutes, *Panoramic View; Waikiki Beach Honolulu; Surf Board Riders; Waikiki Honolulu*; and *Surf Scenes, Waikiki Honolulu* constitute an important historical record that employs an approach to documenting surfing that would remain largely unchanged until the 1970s.

Aesthetically, the films share much with the 'Pure' surfing films that would come later, as identified by Douglas Booth (see Figure 3.2) and, because of that, could appear devoid of the commercial impetus that

Figure 3.2 Screenshot of Edison's *Hawaiian Islands* (1906), a film that is aesthetically close to Booth's category of Pure surfing films

would define the surfing boom of the 1960s. However, while they share much aesthetically, these films were advertisements specifically designed and commissioned to attract North American tourists to Hawai'i. Wood exclaimed that 'It will not be long before the residents of every village and city in the United States as well as across the Atlantic will have the opportunity of seeing life in Hawaii as shown on the screen by moving pictures thus creating a more general interest in our beautiful country than could be brought about in any other way' (quoted in Moser 2020: 506).

The films were exported and exhibited in theatres across the United States, Canada, and Europe and were one part of a sustained tourist drive that saw the HPC establish agencies in Los Angeles, San Francisco, Chicago, New York, and Boston, and 'specifically target Southern California as Hawaii's richest potential source of tourism' (quoted in Moser 2020: 506). Patrick Moser argues that 'what surf historians have previously considered as unconnected or ad hoc events at this nascent stage in surfing's growth – from surfing in film to contests and exhibitions in Hawaii and California – were in fact carefully coordinated by the HPC to create maximum impact on potential tourists and visiting tourists' (507).

Alexander Hume Ford, while usually credited with saving surfing, more accurately benefited from this strategy, becoming the most visible exponent of surf culture in Honolulu when he established the Outrigger Canoe Club. The Outrigger was a private members club that promoted the benefits of surfing and while Ford claimed to have established the Outrigger 'to preserve surfing for the "small boy of limited means," as the club grew it quickly became a racially segregated organisation that catered exclusively to the powerful haole [white] elite in Hawai'i' (Walker 2011: 61). Scott Laderman has argued that Ford succeeded in 'rendering the native population increasingly marginal as the annexations consolidated [the white population's] wealth, power and privilege (Laderman 2014: 19). Indeed, so successful was Ford in his approach, that most contemporary histories continue to credit him as the saviour of surfing, despite much evidence to the contrary. This narrative is writ large in Stacy Peralta's 2004 documentary *Riding Giants* in which they suggest that 'the extinct Polynesian pastime was then re-introduced in the early twentieth century by Alexander Hume Ford, a globe-trotting promoter who set about reviving island tourism by romanticizing surfing at Waikīkī'. This narrative is easily discredited in the work of Isaiah Helekunihi Walker, who argues that 'Ford did not resurrect surfing, as is often purported, but rather learned to surf from Native Hawaiians like George Freeth, who had been surfing and continued to do so in Hawaii during this so-called restoration' (Walker 2011: 15).

What Ford did do was work tirelessly to promote the benefits of surfing to the haole elite, organising various events, and through his writing and photography was instrumental in driving the tourist trade to Waikiki Beach. One of those tourists was the celebrated novelist Jack London, accompanied by his wife Charmian. Ford quickly established a friendship with the couple and Charmian would later describe Ford as a 'genius' at 'pioneering and promoting', saying that he 'swears he is going to make this island's pastime (surfing) one of the most popular in the world', and suggested that through his efforts, surfing would be promoted 'for the benefit of Hawaii and her advertisement to the outside world' (Florida Surf Museum n.d.).

However, it would be London and not Ford who would be pivotal in exporting the sport to California, when he penned a celebration of surfing entitled 'Riding the South Sea Surf'. The piece would appear in the October 1907 edition of the widely circulated *The Woman's Home Companion*, later reprinted in London's book *Cruise of the Snark* (published 1911, referenced edition 2015). The article celebrated the skills of George Freeth, who had taught London to surf, as he had Ford before him, and in his writing, London describes Freeth as 'a young god bronzed with sunburn' and 'a Mercury – a brown Mercury', suggesting that 'his heels are winged, and in them is the swiftness of the sea' (London 2015: 76). The Hawai'ian press dubbed Freeth 'probably the most expert surf board rider in the world' and using his newfound celebrity as leverage Freeth approached the Hawaii Promotion Committee hoping to exploit its transpacific influence and business connections (Moser 2022: 40). Edison's films and the sustained promotional efforts of the HPC had whetted the appetites of native Californians for surfing and the local press heralded Freeth's arrival, proclaiming 'Champion Surf Rider Coming from Hololulu' and 'George Freeth Responsible for Popularity of an Almost Lost Art – To Teach Californians the Sport' (quoted in Moser 2022: 40). The HPC arranged an employment opportunity with conservationist and developer Abbot Kinney, who employed Freeth to help him promote his resort 'The Venice of America', later known as Venice Beach. This in turn attracted the attention of wealthy industrialist Henry Huntington who employed Freeth to help him promote his railway line which ran from San Pedro to Redondo Beach (54).

For all of Freeth's success, these exhibitions led only to a marginal uptake in surfing and it would be another Hawai'ian national who would be credited with popularising the sport, in California and elsewhere. Described as 'the father of modern surfing', Duke Kahanamoku was a competitive swimmer, who, following his success at the 1912 Olympics in Stockholm, settled in Southern California (Nendel 2009:

2433). He began giving surfing exhibitions and a community began to grow, founding the Corona del Mar Surf Club in 1928 – the first surf club on the US mainland. The group held the first surfing competition later that same year, and attracted contestants from Santa Monica, Santa Ana, Redondo Beach and Los Angeles (see Burnett and Burnett [2013]).

The sport continued to grow, and while the surf boom is typically seen as being stimulated by a convergence of media interest, there are structural changes that helped to facilitate the boom. Alongside surf wear basics, such as trunks, shorts, T-shirts, and sandals, two developments helped to ensure that surfing garnered mainstream appeal. The first was the development of the neoprene wetsuit that would enable surfers to stay in the water year-round. Often incorrectly attributed to Jack O'Neill, the founder of the surf wear company O'Neill, the first suit was actually developed in 1951 by the MIT-trained physicist Hugh Bradner, working from his San Francisco Bay Area university lab (Warshaw 2010: 168). When his papers were declassified a number of companies began developing surf suits based on Bradner's designs, but when O'Neill lost an eye in a surfing accident he gained a tactical advantage by branding his company with his own bearded and eye-patched Long John Silver face.

The second was the development of lighter and more manoeuvrable boards, a development that begins in an unlikely place. The father of the contemporary surfboard is widely considered to be Joe Quigg. He was dating Darrylin Zanuck, the daughter of 20th Century Fox studio head Darryl Zanuck, while his mate, surfer and one-time actor Tommy Zahn, was dating Marilyn Monroe. Both Monroe and Zanuck were keen surfers but struggled with the weight of the huge boards, so Zanuck asked Quigg to make her a smaller board that would fit in the back of a convertible. Quigg called the board the 'Easy Rider' but it has gone on to be known simply as 'the Darrilyn Board', a board that is considered to be the foundation for all modern shortboards.

There is a popular perception from inside the surfing community that Hollywood has always been opposed to 'authentic' representations of surfing, a perspective seen most visibly in the documentary *Hollywood Don't Surf* (George and MacGillivray, 2011). It is ironic then that in 1947, it was Darryl Zanuck's daughter who was responsible for the structural shift that would lead to the widespread adoption and commercialisation of the sport.

The Commerce of Surfing's Legitimacy

As Douglas Booth documented, in 1993 and 'after nearly two decades of intense lobbying, professional surfers finally secured an international umbrella sponsor' when 'Coca-Cola announced a three-year sponsorship of a grand prix surfing circuit'. With that, 'surfing joined international soccer and the Olympic Games as Coca-Cola's third global sport' (1995: 200). This bid for legitimacy was underpinned by decades of growth in global consumerism which had created a vibrant market for lifestyle sports. As Belinda Wheaton has observed, surfing had become 'an ever-burgeoning industry around the manufacture and distribution of specialised equipment and related accessories. Wetsuits, sunglasses, T-shirts, sandals, boards, jewellery, watches and surf wax to entice the consumer', noting that, crucially, these accoutrements 'have increasingly become part of mainstream fashion' (Wheaton 2005: 136). Jon Stratton believes that this success can be attributed to surfing being a 'commodity-orientated subculture' which he argues supports the 'two fundamentals of American capitalism, consumerism and individualism' (1997: 183–4). This meeting of consumerism and individualism helps to explain how the ideological countercultural image of the surfer has managed to survive successive waves of commodification. This is not to dismiss or disparage those from within the community who define themselves through this countercultural sensibility; it is merely an acknowledgement that this image has been commodified and now has an economic value in the marketplace. So much so, it has become impossible to wrest the lifestyle from its consumerist roots.

Big Wednesday is a film that resisted the dominant image of Californian surfing, to present something altogether more authentic that was not indebted to the bubble-gum pop sound of The Beach Boys or reliant on the popular image of the surfer as depicted in the AIP Beach Party movies. However, while ideologically different, the film simply adds to, and augments, the popular image of the surfer, and the film's rehabilitation can in part be attributed to the mainstreaming of surfing and the exponential growth in surfing as a 'commodity-orientated subculture' during this period. While the film was still in production, Steve Pezman, then editor of *Surfer* magazine, began producing T-Shirts that featured the logo of the fictional Bear brand from the film, and though these were not official, they acted as a kind of paratextual promotional campaign for the film. After the film was released and it bombed at the box office, rather than disappear, the Bear brand continued to grow with a number of different companies emerging that reworked the logo of the fictional company.

One of the most successful of these was developed by Billy Hamilton, a surfer who is latterly better known as the stepfather of legendary big wave surfer, Laird Hamilton. The former had worked as a stuntman on *Big Wednesday* and claims that one of the producers came to him when the film was reaching the end of production and asked if he wanted to use the Bear logo on his own surf boards. Hamilton recalls saying that he did not want to get in trouble with Warner Bros. but was told that the studio was not interested in exploiting the brand, so Hamilton embraced it. He says that 'We started out with zero and that [first] year we got three million dollars in orders. Next year, seven million dollars. Third year, we're a twelve-million-dollar company. I'm making a hundred and fifty thousand dollars a month in royalties'. He had registered trademarks all over the world for the Bear brand; however, when he hit a bump in Europe a lawyer informed him that he needed the copyright of the original artwork if he wanted to continue his global expansion (Gartside 2021a).

Hamilton enjoyed a strong relationship with Milius, having worked with him on *Big Wednesday* and *Uncommon Valour* (Kotcheff, 1983), and approached him to bring him in on the deal. Warner Bros. still owned the logo and, although it was not using it, the studio was reluctant to sell. Milius sent his assistant, Leonard Brady, a former surf journalist, to Warner Bros. and instructed him to negotiate with the studio lawyers in an attempt to take ownership of the Bear brand (Wharton 1995). According to Brady, he began negotiations at $100 and gradually inched up, levelling out at $5,000, at which point the studio finally relented and sold the rights to the Bear brand to Milius (Wharton 1995). However, Hamilton claims that once Milius took ownership of the brand he began trying to cut him out of his own deal. Milius claims that he was not interested in capitalising on the brand himself, and that it was he who had approached Hamilton's company, the Laguna Beach surfwear manufacturer, JIP Inc.

JIP Inc. was the most widely known of the pirated Bear fashion lines, and Milius claims that he gave JIP Inc. the opportunity to buy the exclusive official rights to the brand for the $5,000 that he himself had paid, but suggests that JIP refused. A fierce legal battle ensued which saw Milius take control of the Bear brand through a profitable deal with Irvine-based manufacturer R&S Trading Co. According to David Wharton, a sportswriter for the *Los Angeles Times*, this deal came at an opportune time, happening just as the surfwear industry was embracing a retro aesthetic, and major clothing manufacturers such as Quiksilver and Billabong were 'churning out flannel shirts and board shorts' (1995). Milius worked with R&S Trading Co. to create a wide array of traditional surf clothing, packaged under the Bear logo, effectively cutting Hamilton out of the business. This brand has continued to grow, producing everything from replica retro Malibu board shorts, like those worn by Jan Michael Vincent's character Matt

Johnson in the film, through to the heavy wooded longboards common to 1960s and early 1970s surf scene, just like those ridden by the characters in the film (Wharton 1995).

Conclusion

This chapter has explored the often-complex relationship between youth culture and its commodification, considering the role that media representation plays in that process, and how that affects our understanding of a film like *Big Wednesday.* Surf culture's transformation from a fringe, grass-roots pastime into a fully commodified, mainstream movement, underscores the tensions and pressure that exists in all youth culture to remain authentic, and the attempts of Milius to intervene in those debates with *Big Wednesday* illustrates, perhaps, the futility of resistance to that kind of commodification. *Big Wednesday* captures an important moment in the development of a movement, presenting the vibrant and vital image of a youth culture far removed from the saccharine commodified Californian adolescent experience, that had been packaged up and exported globally. The subsequent commercialisation and move toward legitimacy as Coca-Cola's third global sport indicate just how far surfing has come and, in doing so, perhaps, make the moment that Milius captured in *Big Wednesday* all the more resonant. However, the acquisition of the Bear brand and production of a range of products highlights not only the complex relationship between commercial interests and authenticity but also the value of brands that are seen to embody a particular idea in the marketplace. The following chapter explores where the film fits within Milius' wider body of work and how it contributes to the popular perception of the director.

4 Authorship and the Star Director

> It is not the critic who counts: not the man who points out how the strong man stumbles, or where the doer of deeds could have done better. The credit belongs to the man who is actually *in the arena*.
>
> (Theodore Roosevelt, 'Citizenship in a Republic', speech at the Sorbonne, Paris, 23 April 1910)

The 2013 documentary *Milius* (Figueroa and Knutson) begins with the quote above, framing what follows as a hagiography: the story of an uncompromising man; a strong man who may have occasionally stumbled; who may have been bloodied by his trials in the arena, but who should nevertheless be celebrated for the battles that he endured and for the stories that he told – and there is indeed much to celebrate about John Milius. His impact and influence on popular cinema is unquestionable, and the romantic parallels one is meant to derive from the quotation are clear. But they are also a misrepresentation that imagines Milius as operating independently of the systems and processes that would critique him and his work. Milius' celebrity and the public persona that he cultivated was formed in that crucible, in direct opposition to the critic, and arguably, the popular image of Milius does not exist without that antagonism. It has helped to consolidate and perpetuate an image of the director as controversial, provocative, and deliberately oppositional, which in turn has served as an extra-textual signature that has become an authorial brand. This brand brings with it certain cinematic expectations and while the majority of Milius' filmography can be seen to neatly conform to those expectations, *Big Wednesday* does not. While the film shares the same heightened moments of excess that are common to all of Milius' work, *Big Wednesday* arguably offers far more sentimental fare than the director's reputation might suggest, and in doing so, complicates established reading protocols of the director and his work. Taking Milius as its

DOI: 10.4324/9780429058295-5

focus, this chapter will explore how the director parlayed his auteur status into a kind of stardom, establishing the parameters of a personality that would come to define his subsequent career and function as an authorial brand. It will explore how this brand has ostensibly benefited Milius, but when his output veered towards something that was off-brand, and altogether more sentimental than his persona and body of work would allow, his established brand and his larger-than-life persona failed him.

The Director as Auteur

The figure of the auteur as an anchoring device was fundamental to early conceptions of film studies; it was also one of the defining characteristics of the New Hollywood. This focus on a singular authorial voice drew upon literary theory and helped to establish film as a topic worthy of study. The popularity of such a perspective was instrumental in reinforcing a narrative in which the art and artistry of a few talented individuals shook up the Hollywood film industry (see Pye and Myles [1979]) and, while there are, of course, elements of truth to this narrative, the emphasis on the artistry of a handful of celebrated individuals usually imagines the New Hollywood as a revolution that was somehow removed from the crass commercialism and industrial practices that had defined classical Hollywood cinema. This is one of the central conceits of Peter Biskind's popular history, *Easy Riders, Raging Bulls* (Biskind 1998), in which he argues that '[a]t its most ambitious, the New Hollywood was a movement intended to cut film free of its evil twin, commerce', suggesting that 'the filmmakers of the '70s hoped to overthrow the studio system, or at least render it irrelevant, by democratizing filmmaking and putting it into the hands of anyone with talent and determination' (1998: 17).

The romanticism that pervades Biskind's account is compelling. However, rather than express a desire to overthrow the system, many filmmakers simply wanted the opportunity to join, or, at the very least, emulate the success that the studio system had achieved. This is certainly a perspective expressed by Francis Ford Coppola on the formation of Zoetrope Studios, which he imagined as an 'all inclusive gathering of talent utilizing the best features of the powerful and productive studios of the 30s and 40s' (Riviere 1979: 40). However, in spite of their lofty ambitions and individual achievements, Biskind presents Coppola, Spielberg and, to a lesser degree, Lucas as archetypes of New Hollywood auteurism, even though each would go on to establish their own studios, and in the case of Lucas, much of the infrastructure on which the contemporary industry is built.[1] While it is appealing to imagine the New Hollywood as somehow removed from these processes of commodification it is a fruitless task in which Biskind frequently returns to the figure of the auteur as a focal point through which to elevate art above commerce. However, to do so, he relies explicitly on an outdated mode of auteurism which must be complicated if one is to understand how contemporary ideas of the auteur can be applied successfully to a director like Milius and what this can tell us about the film industry.

Despite widespread appeal and popular cultural adoption, the idea of the auteur remains one of the most contested ideas in film studies. Warren Buckland condemned the auteurist position as 'a narrowly focused, evaluative form of film criticism that not only privileges the work of directors over other above-the-line filmmakers (screenwriters, cinematographers, producers, etc.) but also isolates a small, elite group of directors, conferring upon them the title of auteur' (Buckland 2016: 2). Stephen Crofts has described the concept as theoretically bankrupt (1998: 311), and Thomas Schatz argued that auteurism 'would not be worth bothering with if it hadn't been so influential', suggesting that it had succeeded in 'effectively stalling film history and criticism in a prolonged state of adolescent romanticism (1988: 5). Nevertheless, the idea persists and continues to hold sway over the popular imagination, influencing not only how generations of filmgoers have understood and negotiated film and the filmmaking process, but also how a generation of directors presented themselves and their work to the cinemagoing public. As Alfio Leotta observed, 'the young filmmakers of the New Wave movement regarded themselves as auteurs and situated their filmmaking practices between Classical Hollywood and the European and Japanese authorial tradition' (2018: 8). Milius certainly conceived of himself in this way, arguing that 'we were very much concerned with making the Hollywood film, not to make a lot of money, but as artists' (Bordwell and Thompson 2002: 572).[2]

This sense of the director as artist underpinned early conceptions of auteurism (see Truffaut [1954] and Sarris [2016]), however, the traditional notion of the auteur has long been complicated by ideas of stardom and commerce. One of the most productive developments in understanding auteurism comes from the work of Timothy Corrigan, who describes contemporary auteurism as a kind of commercial scaffolding that frames one's understanding of the director. Drawing on what Michel Foucault called the 'authorial function' (see Foucault [1977]), Corrigan highlights the branding strategies common to film, which 'often proclaim the filmmaker's name' and function 'as a kind of brand-name vision that precedes and succeeds the film'. For Corrigan these extratextual elements influence the way a movie is seen and received, where studios routinely employ the figure of the auteur as part of a sustained commercial strategy (1991: 102). This emphasis on commerce breaks with traditional notions of the auteur, and while there is much value to a traditional approach (Alfio Leotta's book-length study of Milius spends a great deal of time exploring the themes, style and politics of the director's oeuvre and then mapping the director onto traditional notions of auteur), the performativity of Milius' public persona encourages a reading that recognises that his authorial status is explicitly tied to a sustained commercial strategy and is therefore extratextual. While this does not negate readings that embrace traditional textual notions of the auteur, it does complicate those readings and, in the case of Milius, encourages an assessment of the director as a star and that stardom as the result of what Bazin called 'a cult of personality' (1985: 257).[3]

The Auteur as Star

Milius' assent of Hollywood was swift. He was recruited to American International Pictures (AIP) to write a cheap knock-off of *The Dirty Dozen* (Aldrich, 1967) called *The Devil's 8* (Topper, 1969) (Segaloff 2006: 283) after being namechecked in a *New York Times* article by influential film critic Vincent Canby (1968: 58) when he was still a student. Shortly afterwards Warner Bros. hired him to write an adaptation of the novel *Crow Killer: The Saga of Liver-Eating Johnson* (Thorpe Jnr. and Bender 2016) and a script that would become *Jeremiah Johnson* (Pollack, 1972). Sensing his growing stock in Hollywood, and increasingly unhappy with the way his material was being adapted, Milius wrote a speculative screenplay for what became *The Life and Times of Judge Roy Bean* (Huston, 1972) and began shopping it around Hollywood, hoping for the opportunity to direct. Unable to find a studio willing to take a risk on the untested director, he sold the script to First Artists for $300,000 (Pye and Myles 1979: 178) and the studio brought in John Huston to direct.

Pauline Kael, who had previously namechecked Milius in her review of *Jeremiah Johnson*, suggested that the film had been written by vultures and spent most of her review of *The Life and Times of Judge Roy Bean* in a vitriolic rant against Milius, arguing that he was 'having a flamboyant success in fantasy land'. She noted that he was 'a hunting enthusiast' and that 'he had it written into his contract with Warners for "Jeremiah Johnson" that he would get to shoot the numerous animals that his script (later modified) required be slaughtered'. And suggested that if [his debut feature as director] *Dillinger* (1973) became a hit, 'he [could] probably get a contract to shoot the actors in his next one'. She closed her review stating that 'Milius [was] another of the boys in the "Naked Ape" movie colony' (Kael 1976: 100). However, while Kael was unequivocal in her dislike of Milius, would-be screen-writer, future Scorsese collaborator, and Kael protégé, Paul Schrader was more measured and wrote an incredibly insightful article for the *Los Angeles Weekly News* in which he detailed all of the ways that Hollywood's latest 'enfant terrible' was being discussed in the media (Schrader 1973: 26). He notes that *Newsweek* had afforded Milius star status, while *Esquire* had dubbed him 'Mr Macho', and Pauline Kael had suggested that he was a 'representative of the film industry's "chic fascism" and "amorality" (Schrader 1973) Milius was only too happy to court this kind of controversy, unaware or undeterred by the possible problems of these associations. When Schrader asked him what he wanted as an artist, Milius exclaimed 'fast red cars, beautiful women, drugs and booze'. When Schrader really pressed him on it, Milius simply doubled-down stating 'cars and women? Who wants cars and women? I want tanks, jets, ordinance! Munitions, that's what I want' (Milius, quoted in Schrader 1973).

In these moments, even at this early stage, one can see the kind of rhetoric that would go on to define Milius, and the theatrical larger-than-life public persona that would ultimately overshadow his work. However, one can also clearly see that this is delivered with a wink and a smile and is not to be taken seriously. Schrader is perceptive, and rather than accept these moments as an accurate representation of the man, he instead dismisses it all to dub him 'the master of flash'. For Schrader, 'flash is the art of the moment: the flamboyant gesture, the well-chosen phrase, the deft hyperbole' (1973: 26), and in this moment, Schrader sees right through the public persona to the talented filmmaker underneath. In what would become a prophetic statement, he warns:

> Because Milius is flamboyant, people assume that he is immune to this sort of attack. That's not true. Great flamboyant artists are very easily brought down. Witness Orson Welles, Marlon Brando, Rip Torn. We covet their energy, resent their arrogance. We try to make them buffoons, and if they don't become buffoons, we ostracise them. Flamboyant artists always run the risk of becoming court jesters, that is, they become talk show guests. They are gradually demeaned by their own superabundance of talent.
>
> (Schrader 1973)

In this moment, Schrader effectively predicts the downfall of Milius, over a decade before it would happen. Isolating the flamboyance and performative zeal that already defined the character that Milius had created, Schrader highlights all of the ways that this construction would leave him open to attack. However, for the time being, at least, Milius' star was on the rise and the press was interested in the comically controversial director. An interview given to Burr Snider in 1973 for *Esquire* magazine hyperbolically enumerates his various likes and dislikes:

> John Milius likes: surfing, hunting, *Bushido*, Dom Perignon Champagne, Beluga caviar, John Wayne and Marlon Brando, John Ford, Kurosawa, Teddy Roosevelt, decadence, '*le grande audace*', Patton, the fresh orange juice served at the Polo Lounge of the Beverly Hills Hotel, grand passions, *True Grit* (the book), Stewart boots, Purdey and Perazzi shotguns, Joan Baez's singing and Pauline Kael's writing style.
>
> He abhors (to varying degrees): most liberals, draft dodgers, protest songs, dope and hippies, *The Last Picture Show,* Fellini, Godard and Peckinpah, Hollywood snake types, work, pretension, New York hypocrites, the Sixties, Joan Baez's politics, and Pauline Kael's ideas about movies.
>
> (Snider 1973)

Evident are the provocatively conservative politics that would come to define the public persona of John Milius, a love of guns and hunting, champagne and caviar, all while rejecting liberal ideals, from hippies to the sixties and all that it represents. There is a continuity here in his admiration of the actors: John Wayne and Marlon Brando; of the directors: John Ford and Akira Kurosawa; and of the leaders: General George S. Patton and President Theodore 'Teddy' Roosevelt. One can already see the fascination with 'great men' that would continue to inform his work as a director and, crucially, one can also see the antagonism between Kael and Milius that would help to consolidate the popular perception of Milius in the press.

In the *New York Times* in September 1973, following the release of Milius' directorial debut *Dillinger*, Stephen Farber led a tirade that was as much a condemnation of auteur theory itself as it was a critique of the director. In the article, Farber dismisses *Dillinger* as a 'flat, derivative piece of hackwork' and argues that while there are continuities between Peckinpah and Milius, 'Peckinpah's raw, brutal, misogynous movies are charged with an artist's passion', while 'Milius is a soft flabby director with a weakness for soft-focus blurs, the lyricism of breath spray commercials' (Farber 1973: 13). Farber attributes the elevation of Milius to the emergence of auteur theory, arguing that 'ten years ago the idea of building a promotion campaign for a movie around the personality of the director would have been virtually unthinkable', but that 'since the auteur theory and the media's restless search for new celebrities, have turned the director into a superstar' (Farber 1973: 13). While the article is wholly dismissive of Milius and his oeuvre, even going so far as to ask 'how long will it take Hollywood to realize that the emperor has no clothes?', Farber is astute in his assessment of Milius, suggesting that 'he knows that publicity is a source of power, and that by creating a colourful myth about himself, he achieves a status on the Hollywood cocktail party circuit' (Farber 1973: 13). Indeed, an entertaining anecdote that is often told about Milius relates to that cocktail party circuit, and a chance encounter between Kael and Milius at Paul Schrader's house in the mid-1980s. During the party, Milius reportedly requested a 'conference' with Kael, who asked in reply if Milius, who by now had garnered a reputation for pulling guns on studio executives, was armed. Milius responded by saying 'tell her I'm not armed. But I myself am a weapon' (quoted in Continetti 2014). This one exchange is telling about his persona, and the performativity that underpins it, but documentarians Joey Figueroa and Zak Knutson argue that while 'his politics or his outlandish behaviour may have limited his career, [...] the thing about John, is that he would never mean the things he said. At his core he's a teddy bear with an AK-47' (Harkness 2013).

This construction highlighted here and in Farber's assault is probably best understood as stardom, certainly celebrity, and conceiving of Milius in this way provides a valuable means of reconceptualising the director through the publicity materials that have worked to shape his public persona. Star studies has long established frameworks that readily acknowledge the star as a composite being, a construction, a commodity, and often as the embodiment of a particular ideology (see Dyer [1998]), all which can neatly be applied to Milius. However, established frameworks for the examination of the auteur, even valuable extensions to the traditional notion of auteurism that come from the work of Corrigan (1991; detailed above) and Kapsis (1989; considered below), have failed to fully wrestle with the idea of authenticity. That idea figures centrally in the literature on stardom and celebrity but is curiously absent from literature on the auteur.[4]

Corrigan offers two means of understanding the auteur-star, suggesting that these figures can be divided into 'the commercial auteur' and the 'auteur of commerce' (1991: 107). For Corrigan, the 'commercial auteur' includes many of Milius' contemporaries: Brian De Palma, Woody Allen and, of course, Spielberg and Lucas. He suggests that what defines this group is recognition and that 'the celebrity of their agency produces and promotes texts that invariably exceed the movie itself, both before and after its release' (Corrigan 1991). Here the text contributes to a body of work that reinforces the dominant reputation of the director as the auteur-star, much like traditional readings of the auteur. However, Corrigan's second category, the auteur of commerce, reflects a break from a traditional auteurist position that would tend to attribute any disruption within the body of work of an auteur-star to authorial evolution. Instead, Corrigan suggests that these fissures and discrepancies must be confronted otherwise they risk fragmenting the coherent image of the auteur-star. This also breaks with traditional notions of stardom and ideas first articulated by Richard Dyer in relation to the film star. Dyer argued that 'star images function crucially in relation to contradictions within and between ideologies, which they seek variously to "manage" or resolve' (Dyer 1998: 34). For Corrigan, theses inconsistencies cannot be resolved; moreover, they risk unseating the auteur-star through a destabilisation of a coherent brand image. Conversely, star studies has no such expectation and Dyer argues that the star is inherently contradictory and that the star image is the product of these paradoxes. Central to this is the belief that the star is both 'ordinary' and 'extraordinary', and, they are both 'present' and 'absent'. Essentially, that they are enough like us so that we can relate to them, but that they are different enough to be seen to embody some unique or special quality. As mediated personalities we feel like we know them, we see interviews, and follow their social media feeds and these interactions give us a window into their private lives, albeit mediated.

As Yannis Tzioumakis has observed, the contractual obligations of both director and star demand engagement in a range of public relations activities, through which 'audiences become familiar with the individual's background, interests, personal life, position in the film industry, and, finally, comments on the film itself' (2006: 61). However, for all their similarities, film stars occupy a distinct space in the production pipeline that directors do not. As Dyer has argued, 'stars are involved in making themselves into commodities; they are both labour and the thing that labour produces' (Dyer 1986: 5). So, while directors may be engaged in similar activities and may operate in a similar sphere to stars, they are not typically commodified in the same way. This is a subtle but important distinction that works to underline audiences' expectations in the public relations activities that Tzoumakis outlines; essentially that the star as performer can sustain and endure the contradictions inherent in their image, through the lens of performativity, while for directors, because they are not typically commodified in the same way, there is a greater expectation of authenticity and a resistance to acknowledging the performative nuances of their public persona. Corrigan cautioned that these inconsistencies risked destabilising the coherent brand image of the director, but what we see with Milius is often an unwillingness to acknowledge his public persona as performance, a resistance that resolves itself in the persistence of the caricatured image. While these narratives have a cultural value that have helped to consolidate the sense of Milius as star, they also have an economic value that has defined the parameters of a brand, in which Milius is complicit and from which he profits but also suffers.

The Star as Brand

By any measure John Milius is a controversial figure. He has been described as a fascist, a label that he once happily embraced though now vehemently rejects. He has described himself as a 'Zen-Anarchist' and an 'American Samurai' (see Figure 4.1) – though he has never fully qualified what he means by either of these labels (Farber 1973: 135). He has unapologetically provocative views on guns, war, and American imperialism. There are rumours that he insisted on being paid in guns and that in a script review meeting he pulled a 45-calibre pistol on Dan Melnick, Head of Production at MGM (Ombres 2014: 76). He has joked that he co-ordinated the International Writers Army, which he described as 'the terror arm of The Writers Guild of America', and he even claimed that the Guild prevented him from blowing up the car of Jeffrey Katzenberg (former chairman of Walt Disney Studios and the co-founder of DreamWorks Pictures), joking that this would be a 'symbol' and seen as 'a revolutionary act' (Stayton 2006). These are only some of the stories that surround John Milius. Deliberately provocative and excessive, Milius has actively crafted a cult of personality that has secured his reputation as New Hollywood's greatest provocateur. However, while much of this is clearly articulated for effect, most coverage of the director fails to scrutinise the image and instead favours the reproduction of the hyperbolic story of 'the craziest man in Hollywood' (Green 2013). While it is of course impossible to separate those moments that authentically reflect the actual personality of Milius from those that are performatively amplified and articulated for effect, this is in many ways far less important than an acknowledgement and recognition that this is a performative construction.

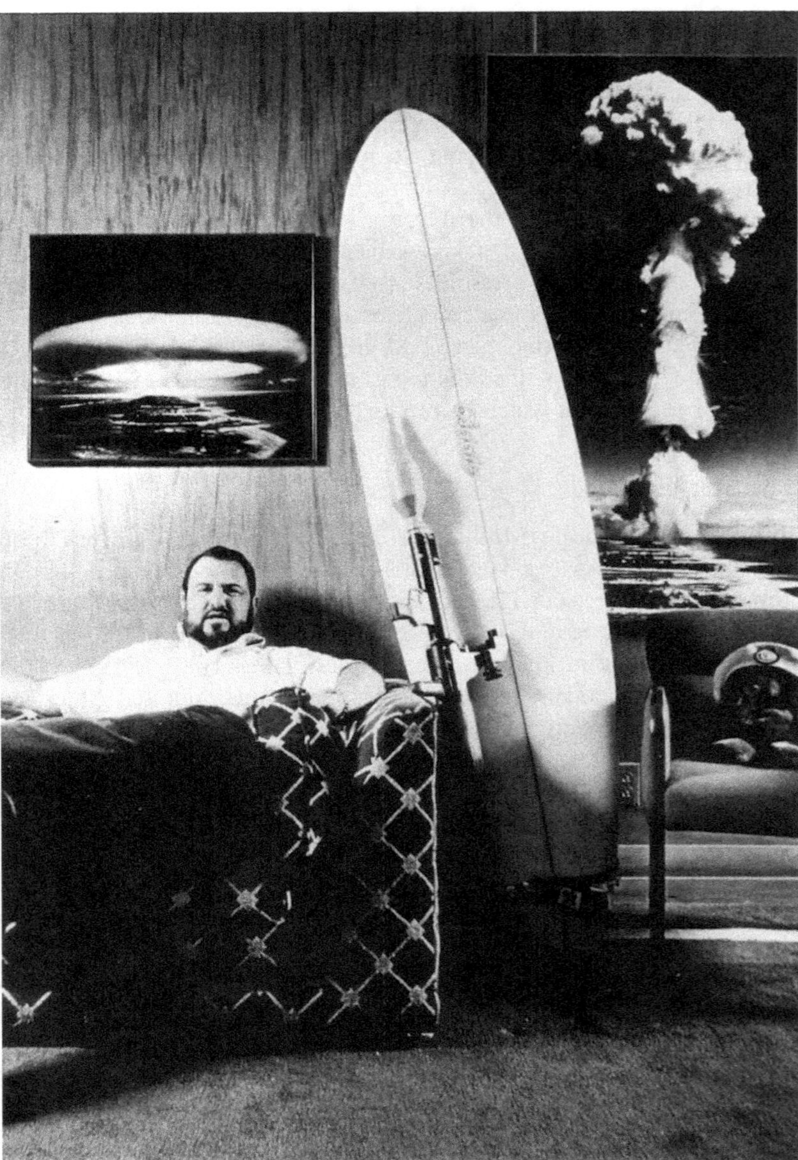

Figure 4.1 A photograph of Milius in his office that captures some of the performativity of the 'Zen-Anarchist', surrounded by iconic symbols of war and surfing (image reproduced from *Milius* [2013])

An exception to this is the 2013 documentary, *Milius*, in which a host of actors, directors, and producers pay tribute to the writer/director and discuss at length the legacy, of both his work, and of the public persona that he has crafted. Steven Spielberg argues that Milius' greatest legacy is as a writer, suggesting that 'Francis [Ford Coppola] couldn't tell a story like John. George [Lucas] is a great storyteller. He couldn't tell a story like John. None of us [could tell a story like John]'. However, when the conversation turns to the popular perception of Milius and his public persona, George Lucas acknowledges the problems inherent here. He suggests that when they were at school together at the USC, it was a little more obvious that the persona was a construction and that Milius was performing a role that was a composite of his various influences.

However, in the years since, many of Milius' own excesses, even those clearly expressed with a knowing wink for comedic effect, have been incorporated into this persona, leaving audiences struggling to navigate perceptions of 'the real'. Over time these stories have worked to erode any sense of Milius the man, consumed, eclipsed, and overshadowed by the weight of this public persona. In many ways this image is his greatest creation, but it has also come at significant cost to the writer/director and, much like Sam Peckinpah before him, Milius became associated with a cinema of violence, and when this converged with his growing reputation as 'the most right-wing film director in Hollywood', it created the pervasive image that would prove impossible to dispel (Medina 2021). Not that Milius has ever made any real attempt to retreat from the persona that he has created, though he has occasionally acknowledged that it is a hyperbolic construction.

The parallels between Peckinpah and Milius are striking and provide a useful means of measuring responses to Milius and his constructed persona. Though Peckinpah eventually shied away from his reputation as mad, bad, and dangerous to know, slowly recognising the harmful effect that his constructed personal mythology was having on his professional status in the industry, Milius has yet to do the same. Gabrielle Murray documents the ways in which Peckinpah's 'anarchic and sometimes violent persona, the development of "auteur theory" and its celebration of the "cult of personality" and the inflated debates surrounding screen violence resulted, for a time, in the "star status" of this director' (Murray 2004: 142). She argues that these elements, when combined with a career spent preoccupied with violence, created the image of 'Bloody Sam' that would prove to be an indelible stain on his life and work. Murray argues that this narrative both helped and hindered Peckinpah, suggesting that 'gentler' works like *Ride the High Country* (1962), *The Ballad of Cable Hogue* (1970), and *Junior Bonner*

(1972) were largely disregarded as not representative of his oeuvre in a narrative that favoured reading Peckinpah's work as an autobiographical reflection of the director's personal neuroses and anxieties (130). Murray also argues that while Peckinpah was 'often insightful about his work, [he] is a fabulous fabricator and an unreliable source, who, in some ways, instigates his own mythology. A drunk, a coke addict, a fascist, a sentimental romantic, possibly schizophrenic, a little man with a big chip on his shoulders' (132).

David Weddle tracks Peckinpah's enthusiastic recreation of himself for the media, removing all trace of his privileged childhood on a sprawling ranch house with elaborate gardens and exquisite décor, to instead, present himself as a man out of time: the rugged cowboy, the dangerous hunter, 'gone were all traces of the rich lawyer's son who had always worn fancier clothes than any of his classmates. The uniform was now complete: dirty jeans, a dusty bandana wrapped around a greying head, and a pair of mirrored sunglasses masking the eyes' (Weddle 1994: 380). According to Weddle, Peckinpah took up knife-throwing as a performative motif that would dominate the conversation anytime a journalist or a studio executive visited his office. He spoke freely to reporters 'of his drinking binges, his whoring and brawling', and 'far from diminishing his reputation – at least at first – it fuelled it (Weddle 1994: 380). Perhaps most significant in relation to Milius is Weddle's account of Peckinpah's romanticising of his (fictitious) past is that in an era that celebrated mavericks and rebels, Peckinpah had transformed himself into a curious combination of Ernest Hemmingway, Hunter S. Thompson, and Wild Bill Hickok – creating the myth of a man who through sheer force of will had taken on the system and won.

It is a similar sensibility that informs the public perception and persona of Milius and, as already detailed, he has been similarly mythologised, both by outside forces and from his own desire to exaggerate and amplify. Perhaps the one major distinction between Peckinpah and Milius is the humour that clearly underpins Milius' public persona. Providing a much needed window into Milius the man, is an article for *The Magazine of the Writers Guild of America, West* which not only challenges the popular perception of the director, it also offers tremendous personal insight into the construction of his public persona. Richard Stayton recalls a lecture that Milius had delivered for the Guild in which, fearing that he might offend the burly director, he shyly asked how he reconciled the inconsistencies in his public persona. Not only was Milius not offended by the question, but he seemed to relish the opportunity to address the elephant in the room. His response, 'yeah, yeah. I love it when people point out these … "You're not a good republican. You're not a good conservative.

You don't approve of George Bush's administration. You're pro-choice. And yet you're a militarist, and a gun fanatic, and believe in the Second Amendment. And consider yourself Roman. I mean, how do you reconcile that?"' According to Stayton, Milius just smiled and said 'I'm a screenwriter. What do you expect? I make it up as I go along' (quoted in Stayton 2006: 27). This acknowledgement of the constructed nature of his public persona offers the most tangible insight into the strategy that has seen Milius become every bit as iconic as his cinematic creations.

When asked about Milius' creative persona, Greg MacGillivray said that Milius 'knew early on that he'd have to become a little bigger than life to get any kind of traction in Hollywood [...] all the Hollywood producers really think about is making money. [...] you have to be memorable. So that's what he did – he created his own persona' (quoted in Pemberton 2015). Similarly, Denny Aaberg has said that his friend was far more than the Coen brothers' quick to temper, battle-hardened gun-toting caricature Walter Sobchak, and although he 'studied war and all these military characters and samurai movies, he had a genuine soft spot underneath his façade' (quoted in Pemberton 2015). This sense of the 'real' Milius pervades the documentary *Milius*, which seeks to celebrate the myth, as much as it attempts to complicate the man. Spielberg and Lucas both talk at length about the man they know, talking with great affection about their friend, before Lucas is cut off in mid-sentence stating, 'and then he's created this ... persona'. USC alumnus Randal Kleiser, states simply: 'he wanted to make himself into a legend' (Pemberton 2015). The effect of this legend is difficult to assess, but in the public consciousness at least, he has become the character that he created, and has established the parameters of the kind of stardom and celebrity reserved for relatively few directors.

The Brand in Crisis

In a study that predates Corrigan's, Robert E. Kapsis makes a case for the 'artist' or 'auteur' as a mutually agreed upon social construction that is the result of considerable effort from 'the forces which influence reassessments of reputation and cultural meaning' (1989: 15). For Kapsis, an artist's reputation was not fixed or constant, but was instead mutable and subject to change and evolve over time. Using Alfred Hitchcock as a case study, Kapsis charts the upward trajectory of Hitchcock, from popular entertainer working in the doldrums of genre cinema to distinguished artist and auteur, through a process that he calls 'reputation building' (1989: 15). While Hitchcock's rise can be read as overwhelmingly positive, securing his place among the pantheon of the greatest directors in history, what one sees with Milius is a kind of reputational consolidation that seeks to affirm his reputation as what Nat Segaloff calls 'big, bad, John', the difficult and uncompromising auteur (2021: vii). Milius has said with relish that 'I have always been on the other side of the cultural war, I have always been an example from the beginning of what was culturally incorrect' (quoted in Segaloff 2021). While this may broadly be true, at a certain point this persona seems more pronounced, more performative, and sees Milius doubling down on the rhetoric that has historically garnered him so many column inches of coverage. In the move from the 1970s and a period in American cinema that had privileged the voice of the auteur, into the 1980s where that discourse begins to wane and the industry becomes reconfigured and defined by profit and conglomeration, Milius is displaced.

In 2013, and after almost two decades in the cinematic wilderness, Milius was interviewed for the web magazine *Film Threat* and was still found doubling down on that image, demonstrating that he was still every bit as invested in the persona that he had created and just how little his thinking had progressed:

> They misread me. They're wrong. I'm really an extreme right-wing reactionary. I'm not a reactionary – I'm just a right-wing extremist so far beyond the Christian-identity people like that and stuff, that they can't even imagine. I'm so far beyond that I'm a Maoist. I'm an anarchist. I've always been an anarchist. Any true, real right-winger if he goes far enough hates all form of government, because government should be done to cattle and not human beings.
>
> (quoted in Lee 2013)

Here, Milius reiterates the attitudes and values that he believes got him removed from Hollywood in the first place, but in doing so, he also demonstrates how unaccustomed critics are to questioning the persona of a director. Corrigan once cautioned that 'today's auteurs are agents who, whether they wish it or not, are always on the verge of being consumed by their status as stars (1991: 49). Milius' star image has eclipsed his work and ultimately proved incompatible with the mores of the contemporary film industry. Because of that perhaps it is better to think of Milius as a writer and in that, as the author of his own biography. In her history of the American Screenwriters Guild, Miranda J. Banks suggests that:

> Screenwriters are storytellers, dream builders, and more often than they would like, simply wordaday hacks. They envision new worlds and the beings to populate them, bringing them to life through storylines and idiosyncratic details. Writers craft tales of heroism against all odds – so much so that they are sometimes swept up in the formula, becoming their own plucky protagonists in epic behind-the-scenes Hollywood dramas.
>
> (2015: 1)

Perhaps that is what happened to Milius, and between pulling a 45-calibre pistol on Dan Melnick and threatening to blow up Jeffrey Katzenberg's car he did exactly what Randal Kleiser said – he made himself into a legend.

Conclusion

The concept of the auteur grew in prominence during the 1970s, and figures like Coppola, Spielberg, and Lucas, often hailed as New Hollywood's artists and auteurs, went on to contribute significantly to the commercial infrastructure of the film industry. While traditional notions of the auteur draw from literary theory to prioritise a singular artistic vision, contemporary interpretations have tended to complicate these ideas by highlighting the role that marketing and branding strategies play in the placement of any director. The provocative larger-than-life public persona of Milius should be understood in these terms, as a flamboyant creation crafted by Milius to gain leverage in the industry early on in his career. This approach has attracted both admiration and disdain, and the intersections between his public image and directorial output have worked to reinforce the sense that the persona authentically reflects the man, a perspective complicated in this chapter. As a comparatively gentle film, *Big Wednesday* (much like Peckinpah's *Junior Bonner* and *The Ballad of Cable Hogue*) exists as an outlier, an anomaly, in a body of work seen to be preoccupied with violence. However, despite this dismissal, there are continuities to Milius' other work which, as Alfio Leotta has detailed, frequently returns to explore themes of 'tradition, adventure, spiritualism, honour and loyalty' (2018: 8). All of these elements can be seen prominently in *Big Wednesday*, and while the public persona of Milius may have overshadowed the film, it remains an important entry in his wider body of work.

Notes

1 In his assessment of the industrial legacy of Lucas and Spielberg, Jon Lewis proposes two waves of new Hollywood auteur, who despite sharing several notable similarities, are also reflective of significant differences both in the way that they approach filmmaking and the kind of films that they make. As part of the first wave Lewis includes Francis Ford Coppola, Martin Scorsese, and Robert Altman, preliminary figures in the New Hollywood movement who Lewis argues 'focused primarily on mise-en-scène and took pride and care in directing actors, set design and lighting, all things accomplished during the production phase' (Lewis 2003: 19). Conversely, for Lewis, directors who came later, such as Lucas and Spielberg were 'almost exclusively post-production directors, experts in sound and special effects and action editing' (Lewis 2003: 19) who would usher in the age of the high concept movie that upended the established the New Hollywood auteurist movement (see Wyatt [1994]). While there is undoubtedly an appeal to the narrative that Lewis presents, Milius sits at the intersection between the waves, complicating the neatness of the narrative.

2 A writers' strike in the early 1970s helped to push the contribution of screenwriters to the fore, giving Milius more claim to the auteurist label. On the back of the industrial action the Writers' Guild determined that (1) The term 'a film by …' shall not be permitted unless the name following that description – be the director or producer – was also a cowriter of the script. This will effectively eliminate absurdities such as 'A Film by Arthur Hiller' appearing at the front of *Man of La Mancha* (although Cervantes would undoubtedly be pleased to let that credit stand). (2) The Writers Guild shall have primary power in negotiating the terms of a hyphenate contract. ('Hyphenate' referring to the growing number of people who write as well as produce or direct.) and (3) The writer's name must be included prominently in all advertising and publicity (Walker 1973: 2).

3 A fear of the cult of personality was among Bazin's chief concerns in his early work on auteurism. Here, he cautioned against replacing careful aesthetic evaluation of the films themselves with what he saw as a dangerous emphasis on directorial presence and an 'aesthetic personality cult' (Bazin 1985: 257).

4 In his study, *James Cagney: The Actor as Auteur*, Patrick McGilligan argues that '[T]he auteur theory can be revised and reproposed with actors in mind: under certain circumstances, an actor may influence a film as much as a writer, director or producer' (1975: 199). In much the same way I am proposing that the frameworks for studying stardom be repurposed in order to understand the celebrity status of the auteur director.

5 Genre and the Male Melodrama

While it is relatively easy to pinpoint the discrete moments in which *Big Wednesday* has been critically reappraised as important, significant or valuable, the road to that rehabilitation is less easy to track and is dependent upon a number of different factors, not least the shifting status of surfing itself which, as already discussed, underwent a radical transformation in the latter half of the twentieth century. However, the elevation of surfing aside, there are two shifting factors that directly contributed to the film's reception upon its original release and that have continued to play an important role in the film's subsequent rehabilitation: genre as a mechanism through which film is categorised for consumption; and the authorial status of the film's director. While the previous chapter explored the complicated reputation of John Milius and the way that this may have in turn contributed to the reputation of the film, this chapter will consider the commercial limitations of genre as a vocabulary through which producers and consumers can categorise film, paying particular attention to those limitations in regards to youth cinema, and films which, like *Big Wednesday,* are not easily categorised by the commercial classifications governing film.

At its core the film is a male melodrama, a sentimental coming-of-age film that prioritises the friendship of three young men as they navigate the turbulent cultural changes of the era. As a male melodrama, *Big Wednesday* sits at a curious intersection in the career and filmography of John Milius and films that are routinely categorised by their emphasis on generic traits. While all of Milius' films lean heavily into melodramatic tropes, they are more readily defined and categorised based on their perceived overarching genre: for instance, *Dillinger* is seen as a gangster movie, *The Wind and the Lion* an adventure movie, *Conan the Barbarian* a fantasy movie and *Red Dawn* as a war movie. *Big Wednesday* cannot be defined in those terms and while it might latterly be understood as a youth film, it did not correspond to

DOI: 10.4324/9780429058295-6

the narratives of disaffected youth that dominated the 1970s and the cinema of the Hollywood Renaissance. Films like *Bonnie and Clyde* (Penn, 1967), *The Graduate* (Nichols, 1967), or *Easy Rider* (Hopper, 1969) prioritised themes of youthful alienation and were part of a wider counter-cultural sensibility that was not reflected in the narrative of *Big Wednesday*. *Big Wednesday* was especially difficult to place because, without other generic tropes to lean into, the film would be understood as a melodrama, and melodrama, particularly in the 1970s, was understood ostensibly as a woman's genre. While this is historically inaccurate, it left the film in a curious hinterland where it was difficult to classify, and therefore difficult to sell. This is a longstanding problem, and as Timothy Shary notes, 'the teen film poses an interesting challenge to formulaic genre studies, if only because this genre is defined not so much by its narrative characteristics (although there are considerable generic similarities among teen films) as it is by the population that the films are about and to whom they are directed' (1997: 39). This chapter will explore the expectations of genre and the associations that audiences bring to film when navigating what can be seen as quite arbitrary categories. It will offer a potted history of the male melodrama, considering its emergence and evolution from the youth movies of the 1950s through to the present day, paying particular attention to the specific difficulties in bringing a youth-focussed male melodrama to market in the 1970s.

Genre and the Weight of Cinematic Expectation

Steve Neale has argued that 'genres do not consist of only films: they consist also, and equally, of specific systems of expectation and hypothesis that spectators bring with them to the cinema and that interact with films themselves during the course of the viewing process' (1995: 160). Usually, they function as a useful means of navigating content, a semiotic shortcut that helps them to make decisions about what movie they might enjoy based on prior viewing habits. But more fundamentally than that, genres are commercial categories that help film producers place their products in the marketplace and play a fundamental role in attracting an audience based on the 'type' of film that they might enjoy. These categories, and the process of categorising film for consumption, can often be quite arbitrary and can leave some films struggling to find a space in a market that often prioritises simple and sellable categories – this was undoubtedly the case with *Big Wednesday*.

In an interview with Roger Ebert in 1979, William Katt discussed the muted reception that *Big Wednesday* had received upon its release and expressed his regret at the way the film had been promoted. He argued that at its heart *Big Wednesday* was 'a really sensitive, intelligent movie. But the studio didn't know how to sell it. So, they decided to punch up the fight scenes, make them more violent, exploit the surfing angle – take the cheap approach. The result was that hardly anyone saw the movie' (quoted in Ebert 1979). Lee Purcell, who plays Peggy, has similarly argued that 'it was given a very inappropriate release, the PR was wrong [...] the film is not a film about surfing any more than *Field of Dreams* is a film about baseball' (quoted in Maloney 2023). Certainly, Warner Brothers played up the surfing sequences in promotion and clearly struggled to place the film in the market, evidenced in the advanced trailers for *Big Wednesday* that accompanied the release of *The Swarm* (Allen, 1978), *Hooper* (Needham, 1978) (also starring Jan-Michael Vincent), and *Capricorn One* (Hyams, 1978), films that all, to varying degrees, prioritise action, where *Big Wednesday* does not (Newsgram 1978: 19). This misalignment could arguably be the result of Milius' reputation, which itself contributed to a system of expectations that created a kind of generic residue that in turn encouraged reading protocols that favoured reading the film through stereotypically masculinised genres, and this prevented the film from finding its audience organically upon its release.

Released in the same year as Michael Cimino's epic war drama *The Deer Hunter* (1978), the second act of *Big Wednesday* plays out over the backdrop of the Vietnam conflict, leading many to conclude that the film offered an explicit commentary on America's involvement in the war. The film often appears in lists of notable Vietnam war films, and Milius' association with *Apocalypse Now* and his own appearances in documentaries like *Between the Lines: The True Story of Surfers and the Vietnam War* (Bass, 2008) has only served to bolster readings of this kind. This is a perspective that informs Joan Ormrod's account, in which she argues that *Big Wednesday* 'is more than just a film about surfing, it is an invocation of American society's hopes, fears and conflicts between 1962 and 1974' that 'tells the story of American involvement in Vietnam through the lens of surf culture' (Ormrod 2005b: 1). Similarly, in 1979 when Peter McInerney was attempting to map what he saw as the emergence of a discrete genre of war film that took the Vietnam war as its primary focus, he included *Big Wednesday* as one of five films that 'each develops images, servicemen characters, and themes infused with the energy and tension of the war (1979/80: 22). Readings of this kind are of course ably reinforced by the public persona of Milius as the gun-toting craziest man in Hollywood, and a body of work that frequently returns to war and conflict as a site of inspiration. However, as tempting as it is to imagine the experiences of Robert Duvall's Lieutenant Colonel Bill Kilgore in *Apocalypse Now* shouting 'Charlie don't surf' over the din of falling napalm bombs, as somehow reflective of the experiences of Jack Barlow or Waxer in Vietnam, it ignores the simplicity of *Big Wednesday*'s narrative and an overarching emphasis on youth and friendship. *Big Wednesday* is a story in which it is not the threat of the Vietnam war that breaks up their group, but instead it is the inevitable move toward adulthood and changing priorities and responsibilities that come with age. In this emphasis, the film presents a fairly typical 'rites of passage' narrative in which the protagonists are caught 'betwixt and between' adolescence and adulthood (Hay 1990: 336) to explore 'issues of autonomy, identity, allegiance and difference in the context of the teenage peer group on one hand and adult society on the other' (Neale 2000: 123).

In an important intervention, Paul Kerr cautioned against explicitly reading film in terms of its socio-cultural context, citing *Big Wednesday* alongside a number of other important films arising from the New Hollywood that had used the Vietnam war not as text, or even subtext, but as pretext for a narrative that was far more interested in exploring other issues. Here Kerr cites *Taxi Driver* (Scorsese, 1976), *The Last Detail* (Ashby, 1973), *Nashville* (Altman, 1975) and *American Graffiti* (Lucas, 1973), alongside narratives in which the Vietnam veteran appears more centrally, films like *Heroes* (Kagan, 1977), *Tracks* (Jaglom, 1976) and *Coming Home* (Ashby, 1978). Kerr argues that 'for all their good (i.e. liberal) intentions, Vietnam is merely a pretext for another anti-war film', concluding that 'Vietnam is rapidly becoming a license for the movie brats to indulge in ambiguity and angst, the twin constituents of art cinema (Kerr 1980: 72).

While Kerr condemns the use of Vietnam as pretext, Colin MacCabe instead sees it as a complete disavowal and is critical of the experience of Vietnam as reflected in *American Graffiti*, suggesting that 'the passing of innocence is reduced in the film to the process of growing up', and that Richard Dreyfuss' character Curt Henderson 'is a writer living in Canada, reflecting on an earlier reality of America that could not be sustained' and that the reality of 'the Vietnam War is repressed and smoothed over' (MacCabe 1976: 21). Unsurprisingly perhaps, given the friendship of Lucas and Milius, *Big Wednesday* uses the Vietnam war in much the same way as *American Graffiti* and is far more interested in the passing of innocence and what that means for the three friends, than it is in wrestling with the realities of the Vietnam war. It is this emphasis on those interpersonal relationships and emotional connectivity that binds the group together that locates the film outside of what in the 1970s were seen to be traditionally masculine genres, and within the realm of the melodrama.

Reclaiming Melodrama

Although considered by Linda Williams to be the principal mode of American popular cinema (1998: 43), melodrama is difficult to define and has a long and contested history through which the term has been variously used to describe a genre, a style, a mode, a specific rhetoric, an aesthetic and a sensibility (see Mercer and Shingler [2004]). Traditionally conceived of in starkly gendered and 'predominately pejorative terms' (Gledhill 1987: 5), the demarcation has often been used interchangeably with terms like 'tearjerker' or 'woman's film' and was historically disparaged as a result of the perceived excess, heightened emotion, and dramatic register that was seen to characterise films of this kind. Christine Gledhill highlights that 'the "classic" genres were constructed by recourse to masculine cultural values – the gangster as "tragic hero"; the "epic" of the West; "adult" realism – while "melodrama" was acknowledged only in those denigrated reaches of the juvenile and the popular, the feminised spheres of the woman's weepie, the romance or the family melodrama' (34–5). However, while these gendered binaries gained much ground in the 1970s, Gledhill argues that the placement of the melodrama as the woman's film had been a 'retrospective categorisation' that not only limited discussion but misrepresented the historical origins of the label.

This is something that is explored at length by Steve Neale in his book *Genre and Hollywood* (2000), where he builds upon Gledhill's claims that the classical Hollywood genres were built upon a melodramatic base,[1] by citing numerous examples where the term melodrama had been 'used and defined in ways parallel [...] with terms like "thriller", "chiller" and even "action adventure"', going on to suggest that the term was routinely applied to what would now collectively be understood as film noir: 'detective films, gangster films, gothic thrillers and woman's films, paranoid thrillers, psychological thrillers, police films or semi-documentaries' (Neale 2000: 180). In *Hollywood Genres: Formulas, Filmmaking, and The Studio System* (1981) Thomas Schatz points to a similar dialogue between what were traditionally constructed as men's and women's genres, arguing for 'male weepies' as a distinct subset of the Hollywood family melodrama. Schatz cites notable examples like *Rebel Without a Cause* (1955) *Bigger Than Life* (Ray, 1956), *Tea and Sympathy* (Minnelli, 1956), *East of Eden* (Kazan, 1955) and *The Cobweb* (Minnelli, 1955) and suggests that the central thread that connects these films and that gives them their melodramatic sensibility is a crisis of 1950s masculinity that sees the male protagonist either struggling with, or reluctant to assume, the role of the patriarch (Schatz 1981: 239) – a resistance that can be seen throughout *Big Wednesday.*

The body of work cited by Schatz is widely considered to reflect the heyday of the male melodrama and mark the beginning of what has been discussed as a period of 'male revolt' (see Ehrenreich [1984]). Described by Joe Dubbert as an 'erosion of individualism' caused by the 'absorption of many individuals into very large organisations, businesses, industries, and colleges' (1979: 242), Schatz argues that 'each of these melodramas is a sustained indictment of the social pressures which have reduced the well-meaning patriarch to a confused, helpless victim of his own good intentions (1981: 239). While prominent for a time, these narratives quickly evolved, and Tom Lutz observes that 'as social roles change over time, and the expectations for role fulfilment change, so melodramatic representation can lose its power to elicit tears' (2002: 192–3). For Lutz, this offers a partial explanation for the waning appeal of the male melodrama as the 1950s turned into the 1960s. Schatz argues that while 'movie melodrama survived into the 1960s, the formal and ideological effects of New Hollywood and the Kennedy Administration's New Frontier affected the genre's development', and that by 'the '60s, the melodrama had been co-opted by commercial television, not only in the "daytime drama" series (i.e., soap operas) but also in prime time domestic drama' (Schatz 1981: 224). Significantly, Gledhill attributes this decline to a preoccupation with auteurism and the rise of genre criticism, suggesting that neither did much to rehabilitate the waning appeal of melodrama (1987: 5–6).

While most histories accept a narrative of decline and a displacement to television, in her essay 'Melodrama Revised' Linda Williams makes a compelling case for the persistence of melodrama as a mode that underpins a range of classical genres. Here, Williams argues:

> Melodrama is the fundamental mode of popular American moving pictures. It is not a specific genre like the western or horror film; it is not a 'deviation' of the classical realist narrative; it cannot be located primarily in woman's films, 'weepies', or family melodramas – though it includes them. Rather melodrama is a peculiarly democratic and American form that seeks dramatic revelation of moral and emotional truths through a dialectic of pathos and action. It is the foundation of the classical Hollywood movie.
>
> (1998: 42)

While her intervention is significant for a number of reasons, not simply for its conceit that the melodramatic mode is the basis for American popular cinema, of particular interest here is that Williams chooses to fold into that mode: *Rambo: First Blood Part II* (Cosmatos, 1985); *The Green Berets* (Wayne, 1968); *The Deer Hunter; Platoon* (Stone, 1986); and *Casualties of War* (De Palma, 1989) – films more readily understood as war movies, and more specifically, Vietnam war movies. While I have already cautioned against reading *Big Wednesday* as a Vietnam war movie, Williams' argument here for melodrama as the basis of action cinema is no less compelling. She argues that 'what counts in melodrama is the feeling of righteousness, achieved through the sufferings of the innocent' (1998: 62), and that 'what makes them tick is thus not simply their action-adventure exploits but the activation of such exploits within a melodramatic mode struggling to "solve" the overwhelming moral burden of having been the "bad guys" in a lost war' (61).

John Newsinger similarly argues that 'all war films are tales of masculinity. They are stories of boys becoming men, of comradeship and loyalty, of bravery and endurance, of pain and suffering, of the horror and the excitement of battle (1993: 126). And while *Big Wednesday* could easily be folded into that mode under this rubric, what is interesting for the purposes of this volume is what is left after this expansion, when the action film has been incorporated into the melodramatic mode. As I have already argued, *Big Wednesday* is not a war film, but it is not really an action film either, although it has moments of physical violence and an emphasis on the spectacular nature of the surf sequences. These moments and the way in which they are delivered could easily be seen to mirror the core characteristics of a typical action movie, but again such a taxonomy would need some expansion. However, if one expands Williams' categorisation to include such films then there is a danger that they ignore the simplest of readings which is arguably more likely. Instead, I would argue that *Big Wednesday* is a drama, or more specifically, a melodrama in the traditional sense of the word. A film that is often perceived to be excessive, that incorporates heightened emotion, and the dramatic register that Gledhill argued characterises the genre and, perhaps most significantly, offers an almost identical tale of masculinity as that presented by Newsinger – a story of boys becoming men, of comradeship and loyalty, of bravery and endurance, of pain and suffering – the only notable absence is the exploration of the horror and the excitement of war.

Andrea Walsh's historic study of the woman's film suggests that 'male-oriented films often dramatize a fear of intimacy (especially with women) and an obsession for individuation ("a man's got to do what a man's got to do") and masculine bonding'. While 'in contrast, the woman's film conveys the primacy of emotionality and human attachment, and often expresses a dread of separation from loved ones, whether they be female kin or friends, spouses, lovers, or offspring' (Walsh 1984: 24). It is significant, then, for all its hyperbolically masculinised excess, that these gendered binaries are not present in *Big Wednesday.* The friends are comfortable sharing their emotions with one another and, more than that, there is a primacy placed on that emotionality and on their attachment. There is certainly a clear articulation of sadness at the inevitable separation of the group that comes through ageing, war (even though its horrors and excitement are not portrayed directly) and death. The themes outlined by Newsinger figure centrally in *Big Wednesday*'s narrative and there is a sensitivity and sentimentality to the film that often goes unacknowledged.

One possible reason for this is the heightened dramatic register communicated by the film's score, composed Milius' former USC classmate and long-time collaborator, Basil Poledouris. According to Laurence E. MacDonald, after the editing of *Conan the Barbarian* was completed, Milius presented Poledouris with two videotapes; one was a copy of *Conan* with a temporary score that Milius himself had constructed from excerpts of Wagner, Stravinsky, and Prokofiev, and the second was a copy of the film without music so that Poledouris might overlay his compositions (MacDonald 2013: 318). Initially intimidated at the gravity of the task that lay before him, Poledouris overcame his hesitation to create something that was just as mythic and grandiose and filled with all the emotional intensity of a Wagnerian opera. *Conan* was the third time that Poledouris had collaborated with Milius, the first on Milius' student film *The Reversal of Richard Sun* in 1970, and the second on *Big Wednesday.* Although thematically very different to *Conan*, *Big Wednesday* is no less epic in its orchestration, and one can understand much about the film's reception and its placement in the market through an analysis of the film's score.

It is a sweeping score that moves between two central themes: bombastic militaristic fanfares that work to communicate the power and majesty of the sea, and a softer, solitary French horn that simultaneously offers a heroic refrain and lamentation that hints at the sense of loss that underpins the film's narrative. In the film's more bombastic moments, it is as if the friends are engaged in a pitched battle with the sea, that they are gladiators competing in a tournament, fighting insurmountable odds. These orchestrations sound like waves crashing down; but then there are more simplistic and minimalistic arrangements that prioritise the Hawaiian folk performances of acclaimed slack key guitarists Keola and Kapono Beamer. All of these elements are present throughout *Big Wednesday* and work to convey the heightened emotion, and the dramatic register that underpins the entire film. The sentiment of the film is simultaneously amplified and overshadowed by this soundtrack, a factor that only serves to reinforce the sense of *Big Wednesday* as a traditional melodrama. As John Mercer and Martin Shingler have observed, within the melodrama 'music is used to mark the emotional events, constituting a system of punctuation, heightening the expressive and emotional contrasts of the storyline. In such moments, music makes these films much more dramatic and, by the same token, less like real life' (2004: 13). Music adds an important layer to *Big Wednesday*, and undoubtedly, when the film is accused of being grandiose and pretentious, it is the heightened emotion provided by the punctuation of the score that critics are responding to.

Jacqueline Waeber's work is particularly important here. A musicologist interested in the historical roots of melodramatic music, Waeber traces the use of melodramatic music back to Rousseau's stage melodrama *Pygmalion* which she believes triggered 'melodramatic technique at a structural level' giving rise to registers that 'remain an identifiable invariant in melodramas of different genres, styles, and period' (Waeber 2018: 191). She argues that an audience is capable of decoding references to other works in the music of the score, and then enjoying those references in an intertextual way as citations or quotations, all of which being acted out in a pantomimic (hence excessive or hyperbolic way). This means that melodrama can often make fun of itself (use irony) while also generating sincere and heartfelt emotion (Waeber 2018: 191). She also discusses melodrama being decentred and locatable in interstices and intersections (crossovers with other works, styles, genres, and modes). While the temporary operatic score constructed by Milius and presented to Poledouris was for *Conan*, it is clear that the same sensibility underpins the score to *Big Wednesday.* Arguably, then, Wagner, Stravinsky, and Prokofiev should be understood as reference points, intertextual citations that provided Poledouris with a melodramatic structure on which he could build the score to *Big Wednesday*, thereby imbuing the film with an epic intertextual melodramatic association.

Selling the Drama in the Long 1980s

At the time of *Big Wednesday's* release, the boundaries of what could reasonably be seen to constitute melodrama were still being redrawn, initiated by Thomas Elsaesser's polemic 'Tales of Sound and Fury: Observations on the Family Melodrama' at the beginning of the decade (1972). While this would continue throughout the 1970s, and into the 1980s and 1990s, it would be 26 years before Linda Williams' influential article would productively expand the category to include what were perceived to be traditionally masculine genres like the war film into the melodramatic canon. In the 1970s this binary was pronounced, and while female-led films enjoyed incredible success in this period, with Barbara Streisand, Goldie Hawn, Diane Keaton and Jane Fonda all topping the box office throughout the decade (Morrison 2010: 3), the films that are typically celebrated from the decade are 'almost exclusively [...] films made by white, male directors born between the early 1920s and the late 1940s' with 'the vast majority of the films in question focus[ing] on white, male protagonists' (Krämer and Tzioumakis 2018: xviii). Recent work has begun to challenge the conventional auteurist discourse that has worked to obscure the creative labour of a whole generation of women (Hunter and Shearer 2023). However, the fact remains that, to date, the majority of the films that have been celebrated from the period were largely created by men and prioritise male perspectives.

Peter Krämer suggests that this emphasis begins to change toward the end of the decade and 'from 1977 onwards Hollywood's commercially and critically most successful films belonged far more often than during the preceding decade to those genres typically preferred by women, that is, musicals, romantic comedies, costume films, contemporary dramas and weepies' (1999: 99). While this may be true, this shift can also be seen to initiate a kind of cross-pollination that worked to strip away the gender bifurcation that had defined the previous decade and informed earlier iterations of film studies. This can be seen most visibly in the emergence of an array of films with a melodramatic sensibility that were ostensibly designed to appeal to a male audience. The late 1970s and early 1980s see a range of paternal melodramas come to the fore with films like *Kramer vs. Kramer* (Benton, 1979), *The Champ* (Zeffirelli, 1979) and *Table for Five* (Lieberman,1983); towards the end of the 1980s, we see an increased emphasis on coming-of-age narratives in films, like *Stand by Me* (Reiner, 1986), *Dead Poets Society* (Weir, 1989) and *Field of Dreams* (Robinson, 1989); and in the 1990s, we see an increase in the representations of sensitive men, often facing difficult or challenging situations, in films such as *Regarding Henry* (Pakula, 1991), *Boyz n the Hood* (Singleton, 1991), and *Good Will Hunting* (Van Sant, 1997). This is a trend that continues into the 2000s with films like *Antwone Fisher* (Washington, 2002), *Invictus* (Eastwood, 2009) and later the *Rocky* (Avildsen, 1976) spin-off *Creed* (Coogler, 2015) and its sequels *Creed II* (Caple Jr., 2018) and *Creed III* (Jordan, 2023). Indeed, the success of both the *Rocky* and *Creed* franchises is illustrative of a consistent appetite for male melodrama stretching all the way back to the 1970s.

Moreover, the critical and commercial appeal of Sylvester Stallone's inaugural outing as the downtrodden pugilist in 1976 offers an interesting counterpoint to the reception and placement of *Big Wednesday*. While perhaps not immediately apparent, the inner-city fairytale of a kind-hearted debt collector who is given a shot at the heavyweight championship of the world shares a number of significant parallels with *Big Wednesday*. Both films are essentially male melodramas, presenting emotional stories that prioritise male experience; both films could be understood as sports films, although arguably surfing serves only as the backdrop for *Big Wednesday*, and boxing plays a far smaller role in the first *Rocky* movie than it does in the subsequent films; and both films incorporate an older mentor figure who in both instances acts as a guide and conscience to aid the protagonist(s) in their journey.

Where the films differ greatly is in the tone of their presentation. Popular cinema of the 1970s typically presented flawed protagonists in hopelessly bleak situations that rarely delivered Hollywood-style happy endings. It was a turbulent time socially, culturally, and politically, and much of that made its way onto the screen, often in urban narratives that foregrounded crime or criminality. It is here that *Rocky* succeeds – as a gritty drama the film adopts an aesthetic that mirrors this preoccupation seen in much of the popular cinema of the period, overlaying a redemptive narrative arc. *Rocky* is a bleak film but where it deviates is in its conclusion which offers an uncharacteristically uplifting ending in a decade otherwise noted for its cynicism. However, even here, Rocky does not win, he cannot win – he simply manages to 'go the distance' with the champ and in doing so proves to himself that he was not 'just another bum from the neighbourhood'. He/viewers would have to wait until the sequel and the dawn of the 1980s to see that kind of positivity presented on screen – but in the 1970s the pervasive sense of cynicism that underpinned the cinema of the period would never allow that kind of celebratory release.

By way of comparison, *Big Wednesday* is not quite so cynical in its worldview, and while its narrative does deal with the trials and tribulations of entering adulthood, it does so from the comparatively idyllic sun-kissed shores of California. While Jack and Waxer do go off to war, we are never really presented with the realities of war, this is not a gritty inner city narrative. Instead, the experience of the friends at home always seems to be one step removed from the experience of those friends at war, effectively insulating the audience from the reality of the Vietnam war. Milius has commented that his film was overshadowed by *Saturday Night Fever* (Badham, 1977), another urban narrative that aside from the dance sequences, offers an incredibly bleak representation of inner-city life. This is certainly a preference that can be seen in the box office returns for *Big Wednesday*, where the film failed to enter *Screen International*'s New York Box Office chart at all, although it was present, albeit briefly, in the Los Angeles chart ('International Box Office' 1978: 39).

The success of the male melodrama detailed above, particularly in the 1990s and beyond, is not only illustrative of the commercial appeal of the male melodrama throughout this period, but is also evidence of a shifting sensibility in the (male) cinema-going public. In the 1990s this shift was particularly pronounced, to the degree that it gave rise to the sociological cliché of the 'nineties man'. Susan Jeffords commented that the 'hard-fighting, weapon-wielding, independent, muscular and heroic men of the eighties' had almost disappeared and were being replaced by the 'more sensitive, loving, nurturing, protective family men of the nineties' (1993: 179). This change was reflected off-screen and contributed to the stereotype of the 'nineties man', the sensitive man who was comfortable enough with his emotions to cry at movies. This shift in sensibility can surely account for two things: first, the decline in Milius' cinematic output and the popularity of the traditional action movie; and second, the rediscovery of *Big Wednesday* as a film worthy of attention. While *Big Wednesday* failed to resonate in the 1970s, it would find a place on home video in the 1980s and then later on DVD and Blu-ray. In the 1980s we see much nostalgia for the 1950s in films like *Peggy Sue Got Married* (Coppola, 1986) and *Back to the Future* (Zemeckis, 1985), as well as male melodramas like *Dead Poets Society* and *Stand by Me*. The latter in particular is notable as a film that utilises a similarly omniscient narrator who recounts the story of when he was young and part of a group of male friends who would also need to come to terms with growing up.[2] In doing so, the film employs a melodramatic trope that was utilised successfully by *Big Wednesday*.

The Fragmented Recognition of the Male Melodrama

In her study of the prevalence of male melodrama since 1969 Amy J. Woodworth argues that 'men's tears are considered rare, and women's tears are considered profusive. Thus, we tend to think of tearjerkers and melodrama as the province of weepy women viewers'. She argues that 'the belief in this rarity is one reason, perhaps, why our recognition of their cinematic equivalent has been so fragmented' (2014: 1) and, in spite of the shifts detailed above, this fragmentation has continued. In March of 2023, journalist Gemma White celebrated the release of *Creed III,* suggesting that the film was creating a 'rise in awareness of the male equivalent of the traditional chick flick [...] a film with an emotional resonance at its core that's designed to provoke tears and big feelings in its audience' (White 2023). While White's article does latterly acknowledge the historical antecedents that contribute to the genre, much of the article is framed as revelatory, as if the genre were something new that was only just emerging. She argues that the genre had 'been brought to the forefront of cinematic conversations with the release of *Creed III*' and that social media had dubbed these films the 'masculine melodrama', the 'male weepie' or the 'guy cry' (White 2023). The article illustrates perfectly the kind of fragmented recognition that the male melodrama has received, and that Woodworth speaks of, where even within a piece of journalistic writing that seeks to explicitly address the lack of recognition of the male melodrama, there is a desire to frame the genre as curiosity, as something new or different.

However, this should not just be seen as a bottom-up consumerist concern and therefore a problem of identification, but also, as a top-down problem of production or more specifically promotion, distribution, and market placement. Milius has often spoken about the pressures that he was under from Warner Bros. to make the film more like *National Lampoon's Animal House* (1978) (Bauer 2015), a film that was released after *Big Wednesday*; and Katt's 1979 interview with Roger Ebert reiterates a similar narrative (Ebert 1979). It seems that the studio was unsure about how to effectively promote *Big Wednesday* and evidently unwilling to acknowledge the melodramatic sensibility that underpinned the film and therefore tried to push its production into something that more clearly reflected the youth market, foregrounding sex and drugs and rock and roll. There is, of course, an irony to the studio's reluctance to promote *Big Wednesday* explicitly as a melodramatic text, while simultaneously seeking to amplify sequences that would prioritise emotional expression and catharsis, elements that are intrinsically melodramatic in nature.

Milius insists that the reason that 'the movie has a huge following now is because it did have loftier ambitions' (Bauer 2015). It is significant that the international market seemed to understand the melodramatic tradition on which *Big Wednesday* was drawing far more than the domestic market. This was certainly the case in Belgium and France, where the film was retitled to *Graffiti Party*, a clear nod to *American Graffiti* (a film that was re-released in the same month as *Big Wednesday* and topped the chart as the highest grossing film of June 1978 (50 Top-Grossing Films

1978: 9).[3] Warner Bros. used the tagline 'la fureur de vivre des années 60' – 'the craziness of living in the 1960s', which is notable because 'la fureur de vivre' was the French title for *Rebel Without a Cause.* In this simple evocation, distributors demonstrated a sophisticated understanding of the genre stretching all the way back to the golden age of the male melodrama, and linked *Big Wednesday* to foundational youth films and 'male weepies' *Rebel Without a Cause, Bigger Than Life*, and *East of Eden*. While *Big Wednesday* would never be sold domestically as a melodrama, it would latterly be reappraised as an important cult film and, in the subsequent decades, repositioned as one of the most important films of Milius' career.

The Cult of Male Melodrama

While traditionally seen to exist at opposite ends of a gendered cinematic spectrum, understanding the reappraisal of *Big Wednesday* as an important cult text offers a productive means of both accepting and resolving the film's melodramatic roots. The cult film, much like the melodrama before it, is a contested arena into which one can include a disparate array of film genres, from art film to exploitation cinema, from camp and guilty pleasures to films celebrated for simply being 'so bad that they are good'. In the contemporary marketplace cult films have become a kind of brand, a pseudo-genre, advanced by the commercial embrace of discourses of auteurism (see I.Q. Hunter in Church et al. [2008]). The success of this approach is evident in the prevalence of supplementary material like the director's commentary – paratexts that present particular films as important or significant. However, alongside discourses of production, it is also important to recognise the role of the audience and the role that discourses of consumption play in the formation of texts as cult. Cult is a highly gendered discourse, that has traditionally been dominated by male viewers. While, as already established, discourses of melodrama are largely seen to be the province of female viewers. This gendered split contributes the sense that these are radically different genres with little common ground when, in reality, what these genres often share is a heightened sense of emotion that can be defined by ideas of excess.

As already noted, excess in melodrama is typically defined by a heightened dramatic register that is seen to differentiate it from other genres. However, the cult movie often shares a similar sensibility and as Mathijs and Sexton have noted, is often understood 'on an affective and visceral level' where '(hyperbolic camp, pornography, extreme horror, weepies, schmaltz, or maudlin melodramas)' are 'defined through their representational and stylistic excess' (2011: 7). The irony in the case of *Big Wednesday* is that, despite Milius' reputation for excess, *Big Wednesday* is not excessive enough, or at least not in the right ways. Certainly not enough so as to have garnered a cult reputation on those grounds. So, while it may have retrospectively been repositioned as a cult classic, this designation is largely extra-textual, as even in its melodramatic excess the film does not deliver the affective and visceral response that one might expect of a cult film. Nevertheless, cult film is an amorphous category, capable of housing an array of cinematic styles and genres, and while Milius himself bears all the trappings of a cult director, aside from the representation of surfing the film itself is remarkably devoid of the aesthetic markers that would usually differentiate a film as cult – key among which is its opposition to mainstream commercial film (Jancovich 2010). Even the film's repositioning in the late 1990s as an important auteurist text cannot fully account for its rehabilitation, coming as it did as Milius' cinematic oeuvre was falling from favour with the cinema-going public. *Big Wednesday* seems to have organically and unexpectedly been elevated from the doldrums of commercial failure to be reconsidered as an important, if overlooked, entry in the director's canon. During this period the film was described as 'not only the definitive surf movie but also one of the very best "rites-of-passage" films' (Strongman 1992: 88) and, in a reading that starkly contradicts its earlier reception, as 'the best film that Milius had ever directed' (Strongman 1992: 88).

In light of this, perhaps the single most important factor in *Big Wednesday*'s reappraisal is its widespread availability, first on home video, and then subsequently on DVD, Blu-ray and Digital Download. In the UK, the film was first released on video by Warner Home Video in 1983, five years after its theatrical failure and aimed squarely at the rental market. The film sits alongside a catalogue of films that were a low priority for Warner, films that had already been screened theatrically, and had already aired on network television and, only after all possibility for profit had been exhausted elsewhere, were finally considered for release on home video (see McKenna 2020). The 1992 release to the sell-through market demonstrates a similar lack of investment, however, the inclusion of *Big Wednesday* in the Maverick Directors series in 1997 begins to mark a presentational shift. Here, Milius' work sits alongside the work of Robert Altman, Sam Peckinpah, Ridley Scott and Ken Russell, reflecting a discursive shift that marks Milius out as an important director. This comes long after the success of *Conan the Barbarian* and *Red Dawn*, films that both contributed to the sense of the director as an uncompromising iconoclast, but that also pre-empted a sustained fallow period in his career. In 2005 the film itself was reframed as important, this time through its inclusion in the 'Iconic Film' DVD series imprint (alongside titles like *Dirty Harry* and Stanley Kubrick's *A Clockwork Orange*). This approach can be seen again in the film's inclusion as part of HMV's 'The Premium Collection', an imprint that repackages 'important films' with an extensive array of supplementary materials. In the case of *Big Wednesday*, a director's commentary, a documentary, and lobby cards and a poster all frame the film as important and/or significant.

What these various releases demonstrate is not just that there has always been a market for *Big Wednesday,* but also how the perception of the film changed since its original release. From a low-risk home video release for Warner Bros. in 1983, through to what has now become a deluxe commemorative reissue. By 1998, perceptions had shifted to such a degree that the film was returned to the big screen at the Newport Film Festival some 20 years after its original release, in an event that brought together cast and crew to discuss the rehabilitation of the film. In an article for the *Los Angeles Times* to accompany the screening, Jerry Derloshon proclaimed *Big Wednesday* 'a wipeout no more' and cited conversations with surfers who believed that the film was 'one of the very few to really capture the surfing life' (Derloshon 1998), while *Surfer* magazine suggested that the film 'makes you proud to be a surfer' (Gartside 2021b). The cult elevation of the film is perhaps most evident in a screening at Quentin Tarantino's repertory theatre, The New Beverly Cinema, with actors William Katt and Lee Purcell in attendance. Tarantino has famously said 'I don't like surfers. I grew up in a surfing community and I thought surfers were jerks. I love *Big Wednesday* so much. Surfers don't deserve this movie' (Marcus 2020).

Conclusion

As this chapter has demonstrated, the failure of *Big Wednesday* to find an audience upon its original release can, at least in part, be attributed to a failure of marketing. Contemporary cinematic trends and Milius' association with a particular kind of cinema meant that Warner Bros. prioritised elements that played only a peripheral role in the film's narrative and, in doing so, they misrepresented an overtly sentimental melodrama which contributed to the film failing to find an audience. While Milius' reputation surely added to this failure, of equal importance is genre as a mechanism through which audiences understand

and consume film, and the gendered bifurcation of melodrama that had taken place in the late 1960s and early 1970s that left *Big Wednesday* difficult to classify and therefore sell. While the origins of the male melodrama can be easily traced to the important youth films of the 1950s (*Rebel Without a Cause, Bigger Than Life*, and *East of Eden*), by the 1970s the heightened emotion, dramatic register, and perceived excess of melodrama were believed to be solely the province of the woman's film, and this too left *Big Wednesday* struggling to find an audience. During this period, many of what might be considered stereotypically male genres were supplanted by discourses of auteurism, and a rhetoric that privileged the artistic voice of the director held sway. It is here that Milius' reputation for excess was consolidated and this in turn created a series of expectations, of both the director and his work. However, the hyperbolic excess of Milius' larger-than-life persona does not translate to the screen, and what we see instead is simply the heightened emotion and generic excess typical of the male melodrama. Similarly, the film's subsequent rehabilitation and reappraisal as a cult classic brings with it expectations of excess, but the 'representational and stylistic excess' (Mathijs and Sexton, 2011: 7) typical of the cult movie are curiously absent also. *Big Wednesday* sits at the nexus of these expectations, caught between the generic excess of the male melodrama, the hyperbolic excess of its star director, and the expected excess that permeates its status as a cult film. Despite the encouraged reading protocol created by this system of expectations, aside from the soundtrack the film is fairly restrained in both presentation and style.

Notes

1 Gledhill cites 'western melodrama, crime melodrama, sex melodrama, backwoods melodrama, romantic melodrama' as notable examples of this cross-pollination (1987: 35).
2 In a comparative analysis of *American Graffiti* and *Grease*, Tom Symmons suggests that 'nostalgia was a dominant tendency in American popular culture of the 1970s', attributing its prevalence to 'a conservative tendency that presented a simplified and idealised view of the era as one of youthful innocence, social stability, economic security and global dominance, and was the inspiration for a significant number of "Fifties" films' (2016: 159). Symmons observes that both films are 'set in "middle class" suburbia and centre upon the subculture and mating rituals of 1950s teenagers as they cruise in cars, go to the diner, and dance at the "sock hop" to a rock and roll soundtrack; all central signifiers of the Fifties' (160).

3 It is ironic, then, given the ways that *Big Wednesday* has been consistently overshadowed by spectre of *American Graffiti*, that in 1978 *American Graffiti* was rereleased, remastered with Dolby Surround Sound for a new generation of cinema goers. Released in the same month as *Big Wednesday, American Graffiti* topped the chart as the highest grossing film of June 1978, and in doing so, Lucas eclipsed the release of Milius' *Big Wednesday.*

6 Youthful Archetypes and the Transition to Cult Stardom

A factor not yet discussed in the reappraisal of *Big Wednesday* is the resonance and/or recognition of the film's three stars, who all experienced career high points during the 1980s. Jan-Michael Vincent appeared in a variety of high-profile films, often cast as the youthful sidekick throughout the 1970s but is latterly best remembered for his role as Stringfellow Hawke in the TV series *Airwolf* (CBS, 1984–6). Similarly, William Katt starred in a variety of roles throughout this period, with early roles as the teen lead in romantic dramas, but is latterly best known as Ralph Hinkley, the substitute teacher with secret superhuman abilities in the TV series *The Greatest American Hero* (ABC, 1981–3). Gary Busey enjoyed the most sustained cinematic success, establishing a reputation as a prolific character actor, and appearing in over 150 films between the late 1960s and the present day, although again, is best remembered for a series of high-profile roles in the 1980s. Each of these actors achieved a level of stardom that afforded them widespread appeal and recognition in the 1980s, but as the decade closed, Katt found himself increasingly relegated to direct-to-video horror sequels, a life-threatening motorcycle crash left Busey with permanent brain damage, and struggles with drug and alcohol dependency derailed Vincent's career altogether, ultimately costing him his life in 2019.

The biographies of the stars offer a curious parallel to the lives of the characters that they portray on screen in *Big Wednesday*; Katt as Jack Barlow, the dependable, if less interesting, of the three, quietly working away in the background; Busey as Leroy the masochist, the unhinged hardman with a tendency for the extreme; and Vincent as the tragic hero, the drug-addled Matt Johnson, who, unlike his fictional counterpart, never managed to break free from the cycle of addiction that came to dominate his life. The decline in the mainstream celebrity of each of these actors can be broadly seen to coincide with the re-

DOI: 10.4324/9780429058295-7

emergence and reappraisal of *Big Wednesday* in the 1990s, and while I would be reluctant to attribute the subsequent success of the film to the impact and influence of their stardom, there is an unexpected dialogue between the two that is worth exploring. Arguably, the youthful image of the three that was captured in *Big Wednesday* reflects a moment before their star personas were fully formed, before age and experience moved them further and further away from that youthful ideal, and before their identities were complicated by the extratextual baggage of stardom. This transformation was negotiated differently by each of the stars, and while Katt continued to trade on a good and wholesome ideal typically associated with youth, Vincent's and Busey's stardom became marked by ideas of excess more readily associated with the cult star – Vincent, through the decay and destruction of his youthful façade, and Busey, by ideas of excess that clearly delineate his early celebrated screen career from his later extratextual persona. This chapter will explore how the star image of each of the actors evolved from the youthful archetypes that had defined their earlier stardom, growing into cult figures and becoming distanced from those earlier images and ideals. In doing so, the chapter will demonstrate how the rites-of-passage narrative that characterises the lives of the three protagonists presented on screen in *Big Wednesday* is also reflected off-screen in the trajectories of the stars. It will consider how these subsequent images differ from those early archetypes and what this can tell us about the formation of cult stardom more broadly.

Theorising Cult Stardom

As Matt Hills has observed, 'work on cult media has often tended to explore the role of textual qualities and authorship', and stardom itself 'has been significantly under-explored in relation to discourses of cult' (2013: 21). The most significant interventions in this area come from Ernest Mathijs and Jamie Sexton, in their book *Cult Cinema* (2011), and from Kate Egan and Sarah Thomas and their collection *Cult Film Stardom: Offbeat Attractions and Processes of Cultification* (2013), from which Hills' chapter comes. Egan and Thomas argue that the term cult star 'has been employed in publicity and popular journalistic writing as a common-sense term, used as a means of differentiating certain actors or recognisable personalities from that of the conventional star and often with the purpose of celebrating their unconventionality (2013: 1). They suggest that 'this differentiation is often based on their perceived excesses or quirks – traits, behaviours or characteristics that are idiosyncratic to them alone, that make them recognisable personalities' (2013: 1). Of course, cult stardom is not limited to fringe performers working on the periphery of a perceived 'mainstream', and Hills' chapter explores the cult star status bestowed on comparatively 'mainstream' stars through their appearances in cult films (Hills 2013: 29).

Using Christopher Lee as a case study, Hills cites *The Wicker Man* (Hardy, 1973), alongside Lee's repeated appearances as Hammer's Dracula, Count Dooku in the *Star Wars* prequels (1999–2005) and Saruman in Peter Jackson's *The Lord of the Rings* (2001–3) trilogy as evidence of Lee's cult star status. While he does concede that these 'mainstream movie franchises [are] lacking in offbeat properties, transgression, underground obscurity, camp excess or exploitation's edginess' traditionally associated with 'cult', he argues that they have 'not discursively disqualified or overwhelmed Lee's status as a cult star' (30). Indeed, he suggests that Lee's appearances in tentpole franchises have been 'downplayed in cult fans' appreciations' and that despite 'mainstream visibility', Lee remains discursively a 'cult star' (Hills 2013: 30).

Hills' work here seeks to differentiate discourses of cult stardom and is interested in *where* and *why* the label of cult is transferred from a film text to a film star, which is one of the chapter's many strengths, but also one of its weaknesses. By prioritising the formation of the cult star through their association with the cult text, the chapter ignores extratextual elements that are often key in establishing a coherent star image, effectively ignoring the off-screen idiosyncratic excesses, quirks, traits, behaviours or characteristics that Egan and Thomas argue make such stars 'recognisable personalities' (2013: 1). In doing so, the chapter fails to fully recognise that the cult star (as any film star) is a textual and extratextual amalgam, formed at the intersection between screen performance and celebrity labour. Richard Dyer's foundational work argues that stars exist 'in the world independent of their screen/"fiction" appearances' (1998: 22) and describes stardom as 'an image of the ways stars live' (39). This is an idea developed further by Christine Geraghty, who suggests that the film star might be better understood as a celebrity, a professional, and a performer, but that this is largely determined by the amount of exposure their off-screen/non-professional life receives in relation to on-screen work, and how much their acting skills are showcased in any publicity materials (2007: 99). The point here is that the film star, and perhaps the cult film star even more so, is the product of extratextual, offscreen labour that goes largely unacknowledged in Hills' work.

Hills' analysis is divided between comparatively mainstream figures, like Christopher Lee and Harrison Ford (conceived of respectively as the cult star operating largely outside of the cult text (*Star Wars* and *The Lord of the Rings*), and the mainstream star operating inside the cult text (*Star Wars, Blade Runner* [Scott, 1982]), and undeniable cult stars like Paul McGann, Richard E. Grant and Rutger Hauer. While these stars do present a range of different 'types' and there may be some degree of fluidity in their characterisation as cult stars, mainstream stars, and/or character actors, and for the most part they have firmly established images that are relatively fixed in the public consciousness. Any work (either on or off-screen) that deviates from that dominant perception would likely be disregarded, just as any work that reinforces that dominant perception will be folded into their established image. As Dyer has argued, stars function through a process of 'structured polysemy', that presents 'multiple but finite meanings and effects that a star image signifies' (1998: 63). Sometimes these elements are mutually reinforcing, contributing to a clear and coherent image, but often these elements sit in opposition and are contradictory. Indeed, Dyer argues that 'star images function crucially in relation to contradictions within and between ideologies, which they seek variously to "manage" or resolve' (34). Therefore, any textual anomalies highlighted in Hills' work would likely simply be 'resolved' through a process of affirmation that prioritises the coherence of the established star image, be that cult, or mainstream stardom.

Despite these issues, the idea of differentiating discourses of stardom in relation to cult texts proposed by Hills is valuable, and an understanding of how cult stars are formed is of particular interest here, not just the idea that discourses of cult can be transferred from texts to stars and vice versa, but also how a star's image can transform over time. This dialogue offers a valuable means of understanding the rehabilitation of *Big Wednesday,* not just through its remediation as a cult text, but also through the reconfiguration of its performers as cult stars, and crucially, the dialogue between these two different processes. While the previous chapter offered a consideration of the process of cultification that *Big Wednesday* underwent, it did so independently of other systems and processes that may have contributed to the cult reputation of the film – such as a contemporary understanding of Busey, Katt, and Vincent as cult stars. This cult stardom reflects the development of the image that had defined their earlier careers, in a transformation that arguably has as much to do with the shifting commodification of cult and the ways in which cult products have been branded, marketed, and sold in recent years, as it does reflect a genuine development in their various star personas.

However, in this context it is valuable to consider the shift from comparatively mainstream stardom, when each of the stars might be understood as 'youthful archetypes', into cult stardom through a process of ageing, commodification, and the consolidation of a particular set of ideas about a specific star. This process highlights an aspect of cult stardom that is rarely acknowledged, and that is that cult stardom is largely the province of the older established actor. While there are examples of younger actors who are discussed as cult figures, they are invariably dead, and the cult label has been bestowed retrospectively and often has more to do with the excess and tragedy that surrounds the conditions of their death than it does with ideas of youth. James Dean is a prime example of this, an icon of youthful rebellion and a cult figure whose status as a cult star is largely the result of the narrative of tragedy. As a performer, Dean was considered one of the greatest actors of his generation, but died before being able to realise his potential and fulfil the promise of the career that was seemingly laid out ahead of him. However, while Dean's screen persona is inextricably linked to notions of youthful masculinity, the cult discourse that surrounds him is not one of youth but of a life tragically cut short (see Brottman [2000] for a greater discussion of this). That is not to categorically say that a cult film star cannot be young, but invariably, lists of prominent cult stars prioritise middle-aged men, and often middle-aged white men. Therefore, if one is to understand Busey, Katt, and Vincent as cult figures, one needs to acknowledge that this label has only been applied latterly, and that in the early portion of their careers, they could be better understood as youthful archetypes.

Heroes, Villains, and Fools: Film Stars as Types

In his seminal work, *Stars*, Richard Dyer groups film stars into categories as particular 'types', and suggests that 'what is important about the stars, especially in their particularity, is their typicality or representativeness', arguing that 'stars […] relate to the social types of a society' (1998: 47) and that often what audiences are responding to in their appreciation of film stars is an affinity or desire for a particular type. Dyer's work draws from the notion of a social type and a typology developed by O.E. Klapp in his book, *Heroes, Villains and Fools.* [1] For Klapp, a social type was 'a collective norm of role behaviour formed and used by the group: an idealised concept of how people are expected to be or to act' (2014: 11). While this is an incredibly useful framework for conceptualising different kinds of star, there are numerous problems with such an approach. Dyer cites both ideological and methodological concerns, arguing that Klapp frequently strays into the realm of stereotyping and that if one is female, black, gay or working class there is little room for them in Klapp's taxonomy. He also observes that there is no discussion of methodology at all in Klapp's work so it is never clear how he arrived at the categories that he did.

Nevertheless, despite these significant concerns, Dyer suggests that 'one can […] *use* Klapp's description of prevalent social types, provid [ed] one conceptualises this ideologically' and 'allows for modifications and additions since he wrote the work' (Dyer 1998: 48). Klapp's work is particularly useful here because it offers a productive means of conceiving of Busey, Katt, and Vincent as particular social types – especially in the early part of their careers and before their images were modified and augmented by the changing expectations of their star personas. This mapping exercise then affords a discussion of how and why their star images mutated. The three prevalent social types proposed by Klapp and restated by Dyer are 'the Good Joe', 'the Tough Guy' and 'the Pin-Up', and while Dyer complicates these categories significantly, adding a valuable discussion of alternative or subversive types, there are still benefits to the core categories proposed, not least that they map readily to, Katt, Busey, and Vincent, respectively, reflecting recognisable categories that arguably enhance the film's contribution to the category of youth cinema.

The Good Joe

The 'good Joe' or 'good fellow' describes a warm-hearted everyman, a good-natured person who, according to Klapp, embodies 'the central theme of the American ethos'. He is 'friendly and easygoing; he fits in and likes people; he never sets himself above others but goes along with the majority; he is a good sport – but […] won't let anyone push him around where basic rights are concerned. Most of the time he is so modest that he seems almost self-effacing: even if he is president of the company you can call him by his first name' (Klapp 2014: 108). Klapp argues that outsiders might 'mistake Joe's equalitarianism, tolerance, and wish to be a good sport for weakness, lack of dignity, unsureness of self, or even vulgarity', but that is because 'there is probably no precisely corresponding type complex in any other country', concluding that the Good Joe is 'as distinctive of America as jazz and rock-and-roll' (109). Perry Como, Bing Crosby, Lucille Ball, Will Rogers, Pat Boone, Eddie Cantor, Bob Hope and William Holden are all presented as illustrative examples of this dominant and uniquely American social type, with Klapp concluding that 'failure to understand the good Joe complex […] is a major source of the misunderstanding of Americans by non-Americans' (Klapp 2014: 109). While Dyer is broadly accepting of the Good Joe as the central American social type, he is also interested in what the dominance of this social type suppresses or conceals and the stereotypes that it reinforces in its opposition to 'sissies' and 'eggheads' (1998: 48).

The Tough Guy

Klapp presents the Tough Guy as part of what he calls 'the deterioration of the hero', bemoaning the celebration and romantic elevation of outlaws like Jesse James, Wild Bill Hickok and 'crooks' like John Dillinger and Al Capone while acknowledging that 'literature seems full of characters interesting, in part, *because* of their badness' (Klapp 2014: 146). For Klapp, the corrupted hero was 'too good to be a villain, too bad to be a hero, too serious to be a mere clown, too interesting to forget' (146). Into this canon, Dyer includes James Cagney, Sean Connery and Clint Eastwood as notable examples of actors who are associated with those kinds of roles and situates them alongside those proposed by Klapp: Mike Hammer, Ernest Hemingway, and Little Caesar – authors, actors, and characters that one might now categorise as the antihero. Despite his trepidation, Klapp suggests that there is much to admire in the Tough Guy, arguing:

> he is like a champ [...] he has the almost universal appeal of the one who can't be beat. Since he usually fights others about as tough as himself, he has a kind of fairness (whereas we should have little trouble rallying against a bully). Another thing that confuses the issue is that sometimes the only one who can beat him is another tough guy – so we find the good guy in the role too, often with little to choose between. Tough guys often display loyalty to some limited ideal such as bravery or the 'gang code', which also makes it possible to sympathize with them. Finally, they may symbolize fundamental status needs, such as proving oneself or the common man struggling with bare knuckles to make good.
>
> (Klapp 2014: 150)

Despite a broadly celebratory tone, Klapp was uncomfortable with the ambiguity of the tough guy type, specifically, with the blurring of the boundaries between good and bad behaviour. While he recognised the qualities and attributes to which one might respond, he argued that 'it is as hero, not villain, that the tough guy is a problem' (2014: 149). He felt that there had been a fundamental change in the American heroic image and, 'a seeming reaction against the tough guy has been noted in favor of a gentlemanly kind of hero, exemplified by Gregory Peck,

Henry Fonda, and James Stewart, aware that the problems of life can "not all be solved by a breezy manner, a gun, or a punch in the nose"' (29). Klapp's commitment to simplistic moralistic binaries demonstrates a lack of nuance that can arguably account for a declining interest in his work and approach. Whereas Dyer was far more accepting of the complications and contradictions inherent in this type and argued that an actor can be seen as 'embodying both the positive and the negative connotations of toughness' (1998: 49).

The Pin-Up

Dyer highlights the virtual absence of women in Klapp's work, citing his problematic belief that 'it is still a man's world when it comes to handing out the medals' (Klapp 2014: 97), and the suggestion therefore that heroism is limited to men. The one notable exception to this is the pin-up, into which Klapp includes the 'doll, cover girl, beauty queen and model'. However, for Klapp this category is not limited to women, including as he does the 'adonis' and 'Mr. Universe' as evidence of a male equivalence in this area. For Klapp, 'the pin-up is found on thousands of magazine covers, bedroom walls and locker doors as a secular ikon', and a 'model of bodily perfection' (39). Dyer develops this work, taking a definition from Thomas B. Hess and his study 'Pinup and Icon' that suggests that 'by the 1940s, the pin-up image was defined with canonical strictness', and that 'she had to be the healthy, American, cheerleader type – button-nosed, wide-eyes, long-legged, ample hips and breasts, and above all with the open, friendly smile that discloses perfect, even, white teeth (1972: 227).

While this offers a useful starting point, this gendered description fails to account for the specificities of the male counterpart, though Dyer does explore this in detail elsewhere. However, rather than present a list of physical attributes that one might find in the male pin-up, Dyer instead examines the conditions of spectatorship, drawing on the work of Nancy M. Henley and her book *Body Politics* (Henley 1977). He suggests that while men stare at women, women tend to avert their eyes and this creates an instability 'when looking at images of men that are offered as sexual spectacle' (Dyer 1992: 123). He highlights the tensions at play here, underlining that as a visual medium, these men are presented to be looked at, but that this 'does violence to the codes of who looks and who is looked at (and how), and some attempt is instinctively made to counteract this violation' and that much of this 'centres on the model or star's own "look" – where and how he is looking in relation to the woman looking at him' (123).

While it is tempting to embrace Klapp's taxonomy wholesale, it offers only a simplistic lens through which one might view the role of stars and stardom within the film industry. As Paul McDonald has argued, while 'on one level, various individual stars appear to share common characteristics, and the system of stardom differentiates performers according to type' (citing 'The Young Male Rebel' and Marlon Brando or James Dean as evidence of that), on another level 'the star system seems to resist the classification of stars as types. The identities or images of stars are of value to the film industry for they appear as individuals'. Building upon the work of Janet Staiger, McDonald (2000: 11) suggests that stars might be thought of as a monopoly and that 'star monopolies are based on a belief in unique individuality'. While I am inclined to agree with both McDonald and Staiger, the categories proposed by Klapp are an incredibly useful place to begin a discussion of star image that evolves and mutates over time, and that transforms – in this case – these simplistic youthful archetypes into something altogether more complex – as happens with Busey, Vincent and, to a far lesser degree, Katt. What follows is an overview of how each of these stars can be seen to map onto the categories proposed in Klapp's taxonomy when they were young and in the early part of their career, before an increased knowledge of their private lives corrupts and complicates these simplistic archetypes in interesting and significant ways – all apart from Katt, whose image remains relatively static as the Good Joe, a factor that can surely account for a declining interest in the star as the decades have progressed. In doing this, the chapter will offer age as an additional element in such taxonomies, complicating further the ways in which they can be used to discuss stardom and its cultification.

Complicating the Tough Guy: Gary Busey Between Esteem and Excess

Gary Busey came to prominence in the late 1980s in a series of memorable supporting roles in action films such as *Lethal Weapon* (Donner, 1987), *Predator 2* (Hopkins, 1990) and *Point Break* (Bigelow, 1991), the latter of which paired Busey with Keanu Reeves in a surf/heist film which functioned as an intertextual callback to Busey's earlier incarnation as Leroy 'the Masochist'. He quickly established an image as the tough guy that would come to define much of his career, and a star image that has been marked by extremes of esteem and excess that significantly complicate an understanding of the actor. He had experienced some success in the early 1970s, with supporting roles in films such as Michael Cimino's

Thunderbolt and Lightfoot (1974) and the Barbra Streisand vehicle *A Star Is Born* (Pierson, 1976), but a career highpoint would come in 1978 when he was nominated for the Academy Award for Best Actor for his performance as Buddy Holly in *The Buddy Holly Story* (Rash, 1978) (see Figure 6.1). While the award would ultimately go to Jon Voight, being nominated alongside Warren Beatty, Robert De Niro, Laurence Olivier and Voight did much to help increase Busey's stock in Hollywood and led to a series of leading roles in the early 1980s.

However, despite this early success as a leading man, Busey has largely operated as a character actor, 'occupy[ing] the small spaces left available around the spectacle of star actors and the central place of their protagonists within the narrative (Thomas 2013: 37). Indeed, his on-screen image has largely been overshadowed by odd, erratic and excessive behaviour offscreen, much of which is the result of permanent brain damage that he sustained in a motorcycle accident that almost cost him his life. This has continued to affect his behaviour and, combined with issues related to cocaine and alcohol abuse, has redefined and reshaped the popular perception of the star. This augmented celebrity image has afforded him myriad cameos, from an early appearance in Robert Altman's *The Player* (1992) to arguably the greatest barometer of cultural resonance, guest appearances on *The Simpsons* (Fox, 2005 [1989–]) and *Family Guy* (Fox, 2010 [1999–]). Both of these cameos present Busey as a man with a tenuous grip on reality, with the former casting him as the host of an infomercial 'Get Out of My Dreams and Also Out of My Car: A Guide to Your Restraining Order'. What is perhaps most surprising about this sequence is that Busey voices himself, presenting an extreme caricature and laughing maniacally as he claims he is simply 'too real' for the 'twelve different women and a small independent film company' that took out restraining orders against him.

While the willingness of Busey to embrace the comedic value of his excessive image is admirable, it is also illustrative of the mania that has come to define him. He has parlayed this cultural resonance into a celebrity career, with a string of appearances on reality TV beginning with *Celebrity Rehab* (VHI, 2008–12) in 2008, *Celebrity Apprentice* in 2011 (NBC, 2008–17), *Celebrity Apprentice All Stars* in 2013 (NBC, 2008–17), *Celebrity Big Brother* in 2014 (Channel 5, 2011–18), which he won, and *Dancing with the Stars* in 2015 (ABC, 2005–24) (see Figure 6.1). Most recently, he appeared as the host of *Gary Busey: Pet Judge* (2020), an Amazon Prime series in which Busey plays an amplified version of himself presiding over a court that resolves disputes over pets! Busey's celebrity image has changed radically since the

Figure 6.1 Gary Busey, seen here in his greatest critical success, *The Buddy Holly Story* (1978), and then in *Celebrity Big Brother* (2014) in a scene that captures some of the excess for which he has latterly become known.

crash and so pervasive is the perception of him as unhinged and unpredictable, that contemporary interviews often begin by incredulously stating that he was once nominated for an Academy Award (McCrudden 2016). However, while his acting career may have suffered since the crash, his idiosyncratic excesses, behaviours, and characteristics have ensured that he has longevity as a cult star. Within that, Busey's career can be divided in two, an early career as youthful, exuberant, and energetic actor who was critically celebrated for his work, and later career as an ageing celebrity known largely for his excess offscreen. In this, Busey illustrates the trajectory his career has taken, mutating from the youthful 'Tough Guy' archetype of Klapp's taxonomy, into a prominent celebrity, noted for excess. In the process, he has come to embody his character in *Big Wednesday*, Leroy the masochist.

The Consummate Good Joe: Reading Blondness as Blandness in the Performances of William Katt

In stark contrast to the excesses of Busey's persona stands William Katt, a comparatively squeaky-clean figure whose greatest success came from a TV show called *The Greatest American Hero* (1981–3). His star image epitomises Klapp's Good Joe, and the actor reportedly drew comparisons from Milius with a young Jimmy Stewart, who, as already detailed, Klapp felt embodied the best traits of the gentlemanly hero (Bozung 2011). However, while there are similarities, there are also significant differences here and while Stewart may have made his name in a succession of roles that cast him as the all-American everyman, there was also a darkness and versatility to his performances that Katt has never had the opportunity to demonstrate. Stewart's performances in *Winchester '73* (Mann, 1950), *Rear Window* (Hitchcock, 1954) and *Vertigo* (Hitchcock, 1958) complicate his nice guy image and lend a sense of depth and danger to his on-screen persona.

By comparison, Katt's performances have converged to reinforce a sense of him as the quintessential nice guy, reliable, dependable and, above all, good (see Figure 6.2). His affinity for these kinds of roles can be seen in *Big Wednesday*, and he has talked at length about being cast as the straight guy caught between the extreme poles of Busey and Vincent (Bozung 2011). While he arguably did a fantastic job and his performance is perfectly convincing, he drew criticism from prominent critic Janet Maslin in a scathing review of *Big Wednesday* for the *New York Times*. Maslin argued that 'the surprise [wa]s not that Mr. Milius has made such a resoundingly awful film, but rather that he's made a bland one', attributing much of that blandness to Katt, and arguing

Figure 6.2 William Katt, as the romantic lead with curly blond ringlets, seen here in *Carrie* (1976) and as Ralph Hinkley, the *Greatest American Hero* (1982), a role that encapsulates Katt's qualities as the quintessential 'Good Joe'

that Milius 'encourages such stiffness in his players that Barbara Hale, for instance, is quite unconvincing as Mr. Katt's mother. This is a faux pas of no mean eminence; after all, Miss Hale actually is Mr Katt's mother' (Maslin 1978: C14). While I am inclined to dismiss Maslin's review as the response of a critic who fundamentally did not like the film, it does raise interesting questions about why she singled out Katt.

Some of that is arguably a cultural predisposition for the dark-haired hero. One of the main characteristics that undoubtedly drew Milius to

Katt for the character of Jack Barlow was his tousled mass of blond curls that seemed to typify the stereotypical image of a Californian surfer. However, while his natural blond curls may have helped him secure that role, there can be little doubt in terms of Katt's longer career trajectory that this likely hampered his cinematic success. Julie Lobalzo Wright has argued that while 'Hollywood has a long history of blond film stars, […] blondness is almost exclusively a feminine attribute. Male stars are rarely, if ever, "blond". They may be described as "golden", "fair" or "romantic", but never blond' (2016: 69). There are, of course, notable exceptions to this, and Lobalzo Wright cites Alan Ladd, Brad Pitt, and Leonardo DiCaprio, alongside her own case study Robert Redford, as deviations from the rule, but she does so with the caveat that these are stars who have managed to negotiate and avoid the feminine connotations that are typically associated with the 'blond' label.

For Katt, this was near impossible, impeded as he was with not just blond hair, but with *curly* blond hair, ringlets that brought to mind child star Shirley Temple. While these were tamed in *Big Wednesday*, earlier roles like *Carrie* (1976) and *First Love* (1977) capitalised on these, casting Katt as the youthful romantic lead. Ellen Templer argues that the blonde female is understood through 'adjectives like brassy, sexy, hot, and dumb, or names like bimbo and bombshell' (2006: 1), and while these descriptors do not readily map onto their male counterparts, the blond male star is no less judged. This societal preference can be seen in a survey conducted in 1983, cited in Anthony Synnott's 'Shame and Glory: A Sociology of Hair', in which 75 per cent of women said they preferred men with brown or black hair, while only 13 per cent expressed a preference for blonds (1987: 387). Katt's negotiation, then, not just of the feminised qualities of blondness, but also the childlike associations of curls, means that he is a relative anomaly as a leading man, and while his appearance may have hindered greater success as an 'A' list star, his appearance and various performances did help to consolidate a sense of him as the Good Joe.

Katt was seriously considered for the part of Luke Skywalker in *Star Wars*, a role that ultimately went to Mark Hamill, and it is interesting to speculate on what this might have done for his career trajectory had he been successful. Both actors share a fairly elfin appearance and are blond (though Hamill more so in *Star Wars* than at any other time, his hair bleached white from exposure to the hot Tunisian sun). However, Hamill's appearance changed significantly following a car crash in which he fractured his nose and cheekbones. He appeared to age overnight, and this shifted the kinds of role for which he was being considered, and, ultimately, led to his establishing a much darker screen presence and facilitating an incredibly successful career as a voice actor. So while there are similarities between the two, the usefulness of these comparisons is limited. Lobalzo Wright's case study of Robert Redford, on the other hand, offers perhaps the most useful means of understanding the perceived differences between Katt and other successful blond-haired leading men, if for no other reason than because Katt was cast as a young Redford in *Butch and Sundance: The Early Years* (Lester, 1979).

Butch Cassidy and the Sundance Kid (Hill, 1969) had been an incredible success for 20th Century Fox, winning four Academy Awards and grossing over $100 million at the domestic box office, and making a superstar of Robert Redford (*Butch Cassidy and the Sundance Kid* n.d.). While always celebrated for his beauty, Redford was able to sidestep some of the feminine connotations of his blond hair and, according to Lobalzo Wright, 'stands as one of the few male Hollywood stars who utilised his blondness to promote an all-American golden boy image that was both romantic and political' (2016: 69). This political dimension drew heavily on Redford's own activism and coalesced to form a screen persona that moved beyond that simple image of beauty and made him more than just spectacle, although that always remained a fundamental part of his star appeal.

While never presented a pin-up in quite the same way as Jan-Michael Vincent, Katt's early films see a similar reliance on ideas of beauty and cast him as the romantic lead in a number of films that defined the early part of his career. However, this image was inextricably linked to notions of teen/adolescent romance, and Katt retained a boyish quality well into adulthood that prevented him from occupying a dominant position as a convincing romantic male lead later in his career. Where Redford had been the all-American golden boy, Katt remained the Good Joe, reliable, dependable, but not necessarily spectacular. There is a simplicity to his image that is not complicated by political activism in the way that Redford had been, and his elfin appearance suggested a boyish masculinity that prevented progression to paternal roles that may have shifted the image in a different direction.

Instead, Katt's image consistently conforms to the archetype put forward by Klapp, a factor that can surely account for the limited reach of his star appeal. After all, being dependable, reliable, and good may be key attributes in helping define him as the Good Joe, but they are not the necessarily the qualities of a film star, and unlike his co-stars Busey and Vincent, Katt has never been prone to the kinds of extreme behaviour that might have elevated him extra-textually. Because of that, under normal circumstances it is unlikely that Katt would be considered a cult star, despite appearances in a number of important cult texts, most notably *House* (Miner, 1986), *The Man from Earth* (Schenckman, 2007) and, of course, *Big Wednesday*. But, paradoxically, the commodification of cult that has taken place in recent years means that the very qualities that may have prevented Katt's elevation to cult stardom have enabled him to be a regular face on the convention circuit, meeting fans who are keen to relive their memories of *The Greatest American Hero* and *Big Wednesday*. Though now in his 70s, Katt's screen image continues to trade on ideas of youthful masculinity, although much of that now is linked to the roles that defined the early part of his career. The most consistent of the three, his image has largely remained unchanged since these early appearances and continues to embody a youthful version of Klapp's 'Good Joe'.

Jan-Michael Vincent: From Pop Pin-Up to Tragic Hero

Ernest Mathijs and Jamie Sexton argue that 'personal tragedy, unhappiness, decline, and scandal are all important factors which can feed into cult reputation (2011: 78), and while Vincent's tragedy was arguably of his own making, it is no less tragic to observe the star's decline from an established box office and television star to a half blind, paraplegic, alcoholic wife beater. A series of high-profile arrests meant that by the time Vincent died in 2019, his reputation as a fallen star whose private life had overshadowed the promise of his early career was complete. Like Katt, Vincent is latterly best remembered for his performance in a well-known television series in the 1980s, but his success on television obscures a long and profitable career on film that begins in 1966 when he signed to actor-turned-talent-agent Richard 'Dick' Clayton. Clayton's strategy was to develop a stable of stars that he would present as male models and teen idols. Vincent was placed alongside future stars Burt Reynolds, Harrison Ford, and Nick Nolte, with Clayton believing that Vincent would be the next James Dean (Grove 2016: 29). By 1969, Clayton's strategy was beginning to pay off and Vincent was cast as the youthful sidekick alongside John Wayne and Rock Hudson in *The Undefeated* (McLaglen, 1969) and opposite Lana Turner in Harold Robbins' primetime soap opera *The Survivors* (ABC, 1969–70).

While largely forgotten now, these roles were significant enough to propel Vincent to the covers of teen magazines like *Tiger Beat* and *Fave*, although his career as a pin-up lasted longer than perhaps it should have. In 1976 he featured in 16 different teen magazines. He was 32 years old at the time (Grove 2016: 29). The release of *The World's*

Greatest Athlete (Scheerer) in 1973 can be seen as the high point of his celebrity, with the film establishing Vincent as a sex symbol that appealed to both men and women. At this point in his career, he was receiving upwards of 5,000 fan letters a week, and his resonance within the gay community can be seen in Paul Alcuin Siebenand's doctoral thesis, in which he explores the industry and the audience for gay cinema in Los Angeles in the 1970s. Vincent sits alongside Paul Newman and Robert Redford as celebrities that the respondents would most like to have sex with, and is paired with Robert Redford and Richard Thomas in a list of celebrity couples that respondents would most like to see engaged in sex (Siebenand 1975: 271). His appearance on this list was no doubt facilitated by the numerous teen magazine covers and his performance in *Buster and Billie* (Petrie and Sheldon, 1974) the previous year, a film that is generally regarded as the first instance of male full frontal nudity in a mainstream Hollywood film.

The 1970s saw Vincent appear in a series of films that, while not hugely successful on their original release, have since gone on to garner cult appeal: 1975's *White Line Fever* (Kaplan), a film generally seen as a precursor to Peckinpah's *Convoy* (1978), 1977's *Damnation Alley* (Smight), a post-apocalyptic sci-fi that partnered Vincent with future 1980s TV favourite George Peppard, and, of course, 1978's *Big Wednesday. Damnation Alley* is significant because it saw Vincent have his first $1 million payday, but it has since gone on to be regarded as *the other* sci-fi film made by 20th Century Fox in 1976, overshadowed by the success of *Star Wars.* Producer Paul Maslansky has argued that 'if *Damnation Alley* had been a hit [...] Jan would've had the same kind of career from then on as Harrison Ford' but his 'film career kind of lost momentum at this point' (quoted in Grove 2016: 119).

Vincent was crippled by feelings of insecurity, and the failure of *Damnation Alley* and *Big Wednesday* only added to those feelings (Dangaard 1997: 59). He relied on drugs and alcohol to perform and needed constant reassurance from the cast and crew that he was doing a good job (Grove 2016: 135). While he had historically managed to disguise these aspects of his life, from 1979 onwards his onscreen work became overshadowed by addiction. By the time he moved to television with *Airwolf,* he was drinking on set, which presented significant continuity problems for the show's producers who had to write episodes based around his condition, which would change from episode to episode (Grove 2016: 157). Despite this downward spiral, by the time the show ended he was the most highly-paid television star of the era, earning $125,000 per episode (157).

However, this success could not rescue a career already marred by drunken altercations and arrests. While Vincent continued to work, his films garnered far less attention than his personal life. A series of very public incidents ensured his name stayed in the press and his second marriage, which had been underwritten by the *National Enquirer*, came to a turbulent end when his wife filed a restraining order against him, accusing him of beating her, forcing her to engage in group sex, and stomping her kitten to death (Grove 2016: 173). His life descended into a series of high-profile arrests for drugs, domestic abuse and three near-fatal automotive collisions, the most serious of which saw him crash his car into a lamp post whilst being more than twice over the legal limit for alcohol. Though he was lucky to survive, he only did so with a broken neck and permanent damage to his vocal cords, the result of an emergency tracheotomy performed at the scene. Vincent then attempted to sue the emergency services that had saved him, and sold his story to tabloid media outlets for the remainder of his life. At the time of his death he had lost his left eye due to an age-related tumour, his right leg had been amputated due to a leg infection as a result of complications from peripheral artery disease, and he could barely talk above a croaky whisper due to the damage sustained in the crash (see Figure 6.3). The looks that had defined his earlier pin-up star image had been destroyed by a lifetime of abuse.

Figure 6.3 From youthful archetype and embodiment of Klapp's 'Pin-Up' in *Big Wednesday* to a fallen star whose private life overshadowed the promise of his early career (image from 'The Tragic Demise & Death of Jan-Michael Vincent', *Golden Rewind* [2024])

While undeniably tragic, Vincent's high-profile demise is by no means unique and shares much with earlier Hollywood stars, most notably Montgomery Clift, whose decline was described as 'the longest suicide in Hollywood history' (Robert Lewis, quoted in Chilton 2020). A contemporary of James Dean and Marlon Brando, Clift was celebrated for his beauty and his talent and, for a time, was considered a part of that pantheon. That was until *he* crashed his car into a lamp post, suffering concussion, broken jaw, broken nose, fractured sinuses, fractured cheekbones, and several facial lacerations that required plastic surgery. The crash radically altered his appearance and the subsequent trajectory of his career. Both star biographies present the requisite 'personal tragedy, unhappiness, decline, and scandal' that Mathijs and Sexton suggest are all important factors which can feed into a cult reputation (2011: 78). Both Vincent and Clift descended into a spiral of drink and drugs; both narratives present the decay and destruction of beauty and of the image that had previously defined their stardom; and, unfathomably, both men destroyed their image with a drunken crash into a lamp post. Karen McNally argues that 'Clift's damaged appearance in his post-crash films becomes a consistent reference to his tragic physical decline, influencing characterization and shifting his image towards cult status' (McNally 2013: 181), and while there are differences, arguably, this same process is true of Vincent.

Arguably, where they differ most is in their status. Clift was seen as one of the foremost actors of his generation, discussed in the same breath as Brando and Dean, who established his name playing the lead against iconic leading ladies, Elizabeth Taylor and Marilyn Monroe. Vincent was only ever compared to Dean in terms of his looks; he was rarely the lead; he was always on the periphery, usually playing second fiddle to A-list stars – John Wayne and Rock Hudson in *The Undefeated*, Robert Mitchum in *Going Home* (Leonard, 1971), Charles Bronson in *The Mechanic* (Winner, 1972), and Burt Reynolds in *Hooper* (Needham, 1978). When he was the lead, in *Baby Blue Marine* (Hancock, 1976), *Defiance* (Flynn, 1980) and, of course, *Big Wednesday*, the films invariably failed to land. However, while Vincent's star was not as bright as Clift's, his fall was undoubtedly greater, from a celebrated youthful pin-up to a partially blind paraplegic who in later interviews struggled to remember how he got started in acting, and could not remember the car crash that had left him struggling to talk.

In David Grove's biography of Vincent, *Edge of Greatness* (2016), he documents how, towards the end of his life, Vincent was appearing with increased regularity on the convention circuit, signing autographs and posing for photographs with fans who remembered the star in his heyday (see Figure 6.4). Grove is fairly disparaging of these events, suggesting that they 'cater mostly to the horror and science fiction crowd; Jan is usually positioned, in this asylum, somewhere between the genre vanguards – the cult movie stars and scream queens, who have made a second career out of this – and the bottom feeders, whose claim to fame is that they appeared in a single film years ago, which they have extrapolated into a career'. Grove concludes that Vincent had signed so much merchandise that he had 'cheapened his brand' and that 'the market for his autographed pictures ha[d] gone soft, like his belly' (2016: 188).

While Grove is keen to dismiss these appearances as the actions of a desperate man, arguably, Vincent recognised the market that had emerged and the opportunities that existed for him to extend his stardom. Capitalising on celebrity labour at a point when his acting career had become untenable. In a telling interview for *The Insider*, when Vincent was asked if he would like to get back to work, he says 'I'm

Figure 6.4 Gary Busey, William Katt, Lee Purcell, Darrell Fetty (Waxer), and Jan-Michael Vincent on the convention circuit at The Hollywood Show, capitalising on rekindled interest in *Big Wednesday*. Image reproduced courtesy of The Hollywood Show.

working now', fully aware of his continued value to the gossip industry with which he was engaging, even if it was only as a cautionary tale (Vincent 2007). This awareness of the continued commercial appeal of his star image and the various ways in which he could exploit it is perhaps best seen ten years earlier, just before his crash in 1996. The marketplace had changed and *Big Wednesday*, once pilloried for its failure, was now being hailed as a cult classic. To capitalise on that Vincent had begun writing a sequel which he intended to pitch to Milius and Aaberg. Unknown to Vincent, they had already begun developing a TV series, which Aaberg suggested 'would have been a starring vehicle for Jan, playing an older Matt Johnson [...] but when Jan got in the car accident, and he damaged his back and throat, John dropped out, and the whole thing fell apart' (quoted in Grove 2016: 178).

Vincent's trajectory from handsome Hollywood pin up to cautionary tale seems so routine that it could be drawn straight from the pages of Kenneth Anger's *Hollywood Babylon* (1998). However, in this context, it illustrates the disparity between his early star image, as the embodiment of Klapp's youthful 'Pin-Up', to his latter celebrity persona, and the ageing alcoholic who had destroyed the image that had once made him famous.

The Cult Star/Text Dialogue

The analysis of each of these actors provides an opportunity to consider the formation of the cult star and their development from the youthful archetypes of Klapp's taxonomy. However, rather than conceive of this as linear process in which an actor is imbued with cult associations because of their appearance in a cult text, this formation can be better imagined as a discursive loop that has gradually and continually reworked and refashioned the popular perception of both the film and its stars. Particularly as they moved away from the youthful ideal that had defined the early part of their careers. Throughout the 1980s and into the 1990s when *Big Wednesday* started being reappraised as an important cult text, each of the actors enjoyed a level of success that was explicitly tied to that moment, the moment of their greatest commercial appeal. However, as their stardom began to wane, the meanings associated with each of them changed: Busey and Vincent, through addiction and excess; Katt, through a string of straight-to-video releases that impacted upon the nature of his celebrity. Mathijs and Sexton suggest that 'a mainstream star [might organically] gain a cult status after they have faded from the mainstream', citing Bette Davis and Joan Crawford, as prominent examples of film stars who had moved from the mainstream to the margins of the exploitation circuit long after their mainstream success had faded (2011: 81), and arguably, the same is true of Katt. However, what one sees with Busey and Vincent is not a move to some marginal exploitation circuit, but rather a redefinition of them as extratextual personalities defined through ideas of excess. Moreover, Vincent's death only serves to further intensify his cult star status, in much the same way as James Dean, Marilyn Monroe, or indeed, Montgomery Clift. This is a process that recasts him as the tragic hero consumed by the weight of his own stardom (see Mathijs and Sexton [2011: 79]). These narratives have a commercial value that is pivotal to the repositioning of Busey and Vincent as cult figures, and the dialogue between this discourse and the one that seeks to reposition *Big Wednesday* as an important cult text is only bolstered by the belief that Busey, Vincent, *and* Katt authentically embody themselves in the film, a belief that is reinforced by the fact that each of their lives has essentially followed the same trajectory as the characters they play in the 1978 film.

Conclusion

One could argue that *Big Wednesday*'s remediation as a cult text sits at the intersection of a Venn diagram that has discursively repositioned Busey, Katt, and Vincent, and continues to rework and refashion the popular perception of the film and its stars. In this discourse and in this context, the biographies of the stars can be seen to function as 'entryway paratexts' (see Gray [2010: 23]), that inform audience readings of the central text by presenting a story roughly analogous to the one presented on screen in *Big Wednesday.* These individual biographies then function as a marker of authenticity, working to reaffirm the link between the lives of the stars and the characters that they portray onscreen – Busey as the dangerous and unpredictable Leroy the masochist, Katt as the safe and dependable Jack Barlow, and Vincent as gifted but damaged Matt Johnson. Through this discursive mirroring, the biographies of each of the stars has then taken on a mythological quality, as rites-of-passage narratives, and cautionary coming-of-age stories in their own right. These narratives follow the actors from the time when they were young when their lives lay out ahead of them and life was full of possibilities, through to the present day. In the process, they reflect the narrative trajectories of their characters in *Big Wednesday* (as the film's narrator laments, 'some got married. Some moved inland. Some died') and bring into even sharper focus the film's contribution to youth cinema, not just as a text, but as a collection of texts and paratexts that serve as a meditation and lamentation to lost youth.

Lucy Bolton and Julie Lobalzo Wright have argued that 'one of the most inescapable realities of the realm of stardom is that some stars endure across the decades, enjoying lengthy and high-profile careers, while others fade away, either into obscurity or crystallised at a specific moment in time' (2017: 1). However, as this chapter has illustrated, the analysis of actors like Busey, Katt, and Vincent can reveal much of the fluid nature of stardom, not as a simple linear process but rather as a continual discursive reworking of persona, evidenced here in their appearance in cult texts and extra-textual discourse. First as youthful actors and then later as cult celebrities. The evolution in the popular perception of these stars reveals much about the mutability of stardom, from the narrowly drawn character types of Klapp's study that defined the stars in the early part of their career, into something altogether more nuanced and complex. In the case of Busey and Vincent, this shift is reflective of a complete break away from the image that had defined them as youthful stars and illustrates a shift into star personas marred by ideas of excess. In the case of Katt, it reveals an actor still defined by that narrow and limited framework, a film star whose extra-textual persona has remained largely consistent throughout his career - the simplistic archetype of the amenable and youthful Good Joe. In all three cases, it is clear that age (and ageing) should be an important factor in any effort to understand the emergence and evolution of cult stardom.

Note

1 Klapp's work was originally published in 1962 and was conceived as a specific commentary on American culture folklore. While its applications are limited now, the social types proposed by Klapp have particular currency in this context.

Epilogue

In 2021 inspired by the groundswell of interest that had elevated the film from the doldrums of critical and commercial failure, Aaberg and Milius revisited their original idea and turned *Big Wednesday* into a novel. While a novelisation had accompanied the film's original release, in Aaberg's words, he had simply converted the shooting script into the past tense and, much like the film, this had vanished without a trace. This reimagined version is presented as a 'deluxe anniversary edition', reframing the film as culturally significant through photo inserts, a surf map of Southern California, an excerpt from the original screenplay, a surf glossary, and John Milius' original 1971 pitch letter to his agent Lynn Nesbit. These elements sit alongside essays from historians and surfers Roger McGrath, Tatsuo Takei, Don James, and William Katt's surf double for the film, Peter Townend.[1] If there were any doubts about the cultural significance of the film, the frontispiece of the book features quotes from Tom Hanks, Steven Spielberg, Quentin Tarantino, and Townend, underlining its importance and its place in film history. Hanks said it was 'the best movie that was made about the joy of Los Angeles', while Townend says 'the story of *Big Wednesday* is real, written by real surfers […] They are universal characters'. Spielberg said simply 'John had done his most personal screenplay […] when I read *Big Wednesday*, I certainly thought it was his *American Graffiti*' (quoted in Aaberg and Milius 2021).

This framing of *Big Wednesday* as culturally significant through its perceived similarity to *American Graffiti* pervades a substantial part of the discourse around the film. When *Big Wednesday* was first broadcast as part of the BBC's flagship cineaste series *Moviedrome* (BBC2, 1988–2000), film director and series presenter Alex Cox explained how the film had been pilloried on its original release, how it had been 'accused of being grandiose and pretentious', with the caveat that 'a lot of good films are grandiose and pretentious', citing *Citizen Kane* as a

DOI: 10.4324/9780429058295-8

prominent example. However, despite this alignment with *Citizen Kane*, Cox concludes his introduction by simply stating that *Big Wednesday* was 'Milius' *American Graffiti*'. It is a similar perspective that informs Barry Langford's assessment with the suggestion that *Big Wednesday* followed the template laid out by *American Graffiti*, 'as the most successful entry in the Hollywood nostalgia cycle of the early/mid 1970s, in which earlier, less conflicted and more purposeful, passages in the "American century" were reviewed from the perspective of the disenchanted 1970s' (Langford 2007: 166).

However, while there are indeed numerous similarities, there are also notable differences too. In terms of similarities, both films depict the end of an era, and, because of that, both have been read as a reaction to the unfolding war in Vietnam. Both are unabashedly concerned with youth culture, nostalgically reworking the experiences of their respective directors growing up in 1950s and 1960s California – Lucas' 'cruising' main street in Modesto, and Milius' surfing 'the point' in Malibu, and both take the experiences and representation of youth culture seriously. Indeed, in a perceptive analysis of *American Graffiti*, Jack DeWitt argues that the 'root concerns of the film, under the light surface, are serious, even grim. How does one face an uncertain future? The loss of youth? How does one confront change or, even, death?' (2010: 47).

These same questions are posed by *Big Wednesday*, but while *American Graffiti* would become a cultural touchstone that continues to dominate any discussion of the youth-oriented cinema in the New Hollywood, inspiring a slew of nostalgia-driven youth cinema imitators, from *Animal House* (Landis, 1978), to *The Wanderers* (Kaufman, 1979), and later, *Dazed and Confused* (Linklater, 1993), *Big Wednesday* failed to resonate on that level. There are any number of possible reasons for this, but arguably the greatest of these is that *Big Wednesday* is far less *obvious* as a youth film. That is not to say that it is not an important film that has relevant things to say about youth, and about the ways in which youth cultures are represented on screen, rather that it approaches the subject matter in a very different way compared to staples of the youth film genre, including *American Graffiti*. Indeed, the appeals to popular youth culture seen in *American Graffiti*, most evident in the strategic deployment of pop music of the period, are largely absent from *Big Wednesday*. As already demonstrated, this resistance was far more about Milius' desire to present what he felt was an authentic reflection of his experiences as a young man surfing in Malibu, before the commodification of the youth culture that he loved so much.

The result of this resistance is that the film has a universality that is not indelibly tied to one particular period (as is the case with *American Graffiti*) and, because of that, has been able to speak to successive generations of cinemagoers as an important and authentic lamentation to youth lost. It *has* important things to say about youth, about friendship, and about ageing, but also about sentiment and nostalgia, and how these ideas are communicated. These are big ideas that deserve attention, another reason, perhaps, that the film keeps being rediscovered by successive generations. In *Variety*'s dismissive review of *Big Wednesday* in 1977 the reviewer said 'a rubber stamp wouldn't do for John Milius. So he took a sledgehammer and pounded important all over *Big Wednesday.* This film […] has been branded major statement and it's got big ideas about adolescence, friendship and the 1960s' (*Variety* staff 1977). But it is perhaps because of these ambitions that the film will always have a place in the canon of youth film.

Note

1 In October 2023, Peter Townend's 'Bear' surfboard was auctioned off and sold for $20,000 ('1977 BEAR …' 2023)

Bibliography

'1977 BEAR Big Wednesday Jack Barlow for PT by Mike Perry' (2023) *Californian Gold Surf Auction*, online, https://auctions.thevintagesurfauctions.com/lots/view/1-6EG4E7/1977-bear-big-wednesday-jack-barlow-for-pt-by-mike-perry.

'50 Top-Grossing Films' (1978) *Variety*, 7 June, p. 9.s

Aaberg, D. (1973) 'No Pants Mance,' *Tracks Magazine*, April, pp. n/a.

Aaberg, D. and Milius, J. (2021) *Big Wednesday: Deluxe Anniversary Edition*, Los Angeles, CA: Rare Bird Books.

Anger, K. (1998) *Hollywood Babylon*, New York, NY: Bantam Doubleday Dell.

Antunes, F. (2017) 'Rethinking PG-13: Ratings and the Boundaries of Childhood and Horror,' *Journal of Film and Video*, Vol. 69, No. 1, Spring, pp. 27–43.

Arseneau, A. (2007) 'Red Dawn: Collector's Edition,' *DVD Verdict*, online, 6 August, https://web.archive.org/web/20100706165422/http://www.dvdverdict.com/reviews/reddawnce.php.

Associated Press (2004) 'PG-13 at 20: How "Indiana" Remade Films,' *Today*, online, 13 September, https://www.today.com/popculture/pg-13-20-how-indiana-remade-films-wbna5798549.

Banks, M.J. (2015) *The Writers: A History of American Screenwriters and Their Guild*, New Brunswick, NJ: Rutgers University Press.

Bart, P. (1990) *Fade out: The Calamitous Final Days of MGM*, New York: William Morrow & Co.

Bauer, E. (2015) '"I Was Never Conscious of My Screenplays Having Any Acts. It's All Bullshit" – John Milius,' *Creative Screenwriting*, online, 11 February, https://creativescreenwriting.com/i-was-never-conscious-of-my-screenplays-having-any-acts-its-all-bullshit-john-milius/.

Baxter, J. (2000) *George Lucas: A Biography*, London: HarperCollins.

Bazin, A. (1985) 'Andre Bazin: On the Politique des Auteurs,' in J. Hillier (ed) *Cahiers du Cinema, the 1950s: Neo-Realism, Hollywood, New Wave*, Cambridge, MA: Harvard University Press, pp. 248–259.

Biskind, P. (1998) *Easy Riders Raging Bulls: How the Sex-Drugs-and-Rock 'N Roll Generation Saved Hollywood*, London: Bloomsbury.

Blacker, I.R. (1986) *The Elements of Screenwriting: A Guide for Film and Television Writing*, New York, NY: Collier Macmillan.

Bolton, L. and Wright, J.L. (2017) *Lasting Screen Stars: Images That Fade and Personas That Endure*, Basingstoke: Palgrave Macmillan.

Booth, D. (1996) 'Surfing Films and Videos: Adolescent Fun, Alternative Lifestyle, Adventure Industry,' *Journal of Sport History*, Vol. 23, No. 3, pp. 313–327.

Booth, D. (1995) 'Ambiguities in Pleasure and Discipline: The Development of Competitive Surfing,' *Journal of Sport History*, Vol. 22, No. 3, Fall, pp. 189–206.

Bordwell, D. and Thompson, K. (2002) *Film History: An Introduction*, 2nd edition, Boston, MA: McGraw Hill Higher Education.

Bozung, J. (2011) '14 William Katt,' Film Interviews #4 (2004–2014), online, https://archive.org/details/film-interviews-4/William+Katt.mp3.

Brottman, M. (2000) 'Star Cults/Cult Stars: Cinema, Psychosis, Celebrity, Death,' in X. Mendik and G. Harper (eds) *Unruly Pleasures: The Cult Film and Its Critics*, Surrey: FAB Press, pp. 105–119.

Buckland, W. (2016) 'La Politique des Auteurs in British Film Studies: Traditional versus Structural Approaches' Mise au point 8, online, https://journals.openedition.org/map/2042.

Budd, M. (1976) 'A Home in the Wilderness: Visual Imagery in John Ford's Westerns,' *Cinema Journal*, Vol. 16, No. 1, Autumn, pp. 62–75.

Burnett, C. and Burnett, P. (2013) *Surfing Newport Beach: The Glory Days of Corona Del Mar*, Mount Pleasant, SC: Arcadia Publishing.

'*Butch Cassidy and the Sundance Kid*' (no date) *The Numbers*, online, https://www.the-numbers.com/movie/Butch-Cassidy-and-the-Sundance-Kid#tab=summary.

Campbell, J. (2012) *The Hero with a Thousand Faces*, Novato, CA: New World Library.

Canby, V. (1982) '"*Poltergeist*" from Spielberg,' *New York Times*, 4 June, p. C16.

Canby, V. (1968) 'Honored Student Movies Shown Here,' *New York Times*, 18 April, p. 58.

Chilton, M. (2020) '"The Longest Suicide in Hollywood History": Who Was the Real Montgomery Clift?,' *Telegraph*, online, 19 October, https://www.telegraph.co.uk/films/0/longest-suicide-hollywood-history-real-montgomery-clift/.

Church, D., Hills, M., Hunter, I.Q., Kleinhans, C., Koven, M.J., Mathijs, E., Rosenbaum, J. and Weinstock, J.A. (2008) 'Cult Film: A Critical Symposium (Web Edition),' *Cineaste*, Vol. 34, No. 1, https://www.cineaste.com/winter2008/cult-film-a-critical-symposium.

Comer, K. (2004) 'Wanting to Be Lisa: Generational Rifts, Girl Power and the Globalisation of Surf Culture,' in N. Campbell (ed) *American Youth Cultures*, Edinburgh: Edinburgh University Press, pp. 237–265.

Continetti, M. (2014) 'Hollywood Renegade,' *National Review*, online, 27 December, https://www.nationalreview.com/2014/12/hollywood-renegade-matthew-continetti.

Cook, J. (1784) *A Voyage to the Pacific Ocean, 1776–1780, 3 Vols*, Dublin: Admiralty.

Cook, P. (2005) *Screening the Past: Memory and Nostalgia in Film*, London: Routledge.

Corrigan, T. (1991) *A Cinema Without Walls: Movies and Culture after Vietnam*, London: Routledge.

Cox, A. (1988) '*Big Wednesday* Intoduction,' *Moviedrome*, BBC2, 5 June, 10:50.

Crofts, S. (1998) 'Authorship and Hollywood,' in J. Hill and P. Church Gibson (eds) *The Oxford Guide to Film Studies*, Oxford: Oxford University Press, pp. 310–324.

Dangaard, C. (1997) 'Danger: Falling Idol,' *Los Angeles Magazine*, March, pp. 54–64.

D'Arcy, D. (2001) 'Go Ahead, Pinko Liberals, Make My Day,' *Guardian*, online, 8 November, https://www.theguardian.com/film/2001/nov/08/artsfeatures.

Derloshon, J. (1998) 'A Wipeout No More,' *Los Angeles Times*, online, 18 June, https://www.latimes.com/archives/la-xpm-1998-jun-18-ca-61037-story.html.

DeWitt, J. (2010) 'Cars and Culture: The Cars of "American Graffiti",' *The American Poetry Review*, Vol. 39, No. 5, September/October, pp. 47–50.

Doherty, T. (2002) *Teenagers and Teenpics: The Juvenilization of American Movies in the 1950s*, 2nd edition, Philadelphia, PA: Temple University Press.

Driscoll, C. (2011) *Teen Film: A Critical Introduction*, London: Bloomsbury.

Dubbert, J.L. (1979) *A Man's Place: Masculinity in Transition*, Englewood Cliffs, NJ: Prentice Hall.

Dyer, R. (1998) *Stars*, London: British Film Institute.

Dyer, R. (1992) *Only Entertainment*, London: Routledge.

Dyer, R. (1986) *Heavenly Bodies: Film Stars and Society*, New York, NY: St. Martin's Press.

Ebert, R. (1979) 'Interview with William Katt,' rogerebert.com, online, 3 June, https://www.rogerebert.com/interviews/interview-with-william-katt.

Egan, K. and Thomas, S. (2013) (eds) *Cult Film Stardom: Offbeat Attractions and Processes of Cultification*, London: Palgrave Macmillan.

Egan, K. and Thomas, S. (2013) 'Introduction: Star-Making Cult-Making and Forms of Authenticity,' in K. Egan and S. Thomas (eds) *Cult Film Stardom: Offbeat Attractions and Processes of Cultification*, London: Palgrave Macmillan, pp. 1–17.

Ehrenreich, B. (1984) *The Hearts of Men: American Dreams and the Flight from Commitment*, New York, NY: Anchor Books.

Elsaesser, T. (1972) 'Tales of Sound and Fury: Observations on the Family Melodrama'. in M. Landy (ed) *Imitations of Life: A Reader on Film and Television Melodrama*, Detroit, MI: Wayne State University Press, pp. 68–92.

Farber, S. (1973) 'What's so Super about This Superdirector?,' *New York Times*, 16 September, p. 135.

Fleming Jnr., M. (2010) 'How Spielberg and Lucas Caught the Surfing Bug (… and Waved Goodbye to Points on "Close Encounters" & "Star Wars"),' *Deadline*, online, 12 May, https://deadline.com/2010/05/how-steven-spielberg-and-george-lucas-caught-surf-bug-and-waved-bye-to-points-on-close-encounters-and-star-wars-39792.

Florida Surf Museum (no date) 'Alexander Hume Ford,' online, https://floridasurfmuseum.org/kahunas/alexander-hume-ford.

Foucault, M. (1977) '"The Author Function." Excerpt from "What Is an Author?"' in D.F. Bouchard and S. Simon (eds) *Language, Counter-Memory, Practice*, Ithaca, NY: Cornell University Press, pp. 124–127.

Frank, T. (1997) *The Conquest of Cool*, Chicago, IL: University of Chicago Press.

Freytag, G. (2004) *Technique of the Drama: An Exposition of Dramatic Composition and Art*, Forest Grove, OR: University Press of the Pacific.

Gallagher, J.A. (1989) 'John Milius,' in *Film Directors on Directing*, New York, NY: Kampmann & Company, pp. 169–181.

Gartside, L. (2021a) '*Big Wednesday*, Billy Hamilton and the Strange Birth of Bear Surfboards,' *Wavelength Magazine*, online, 2 July, https://wavelengthmag.com/big-wednesday-billy-hamilton-and-the-strange-birth-of-bear-surfboards/.

Gartside, L. (2021b) 'Behind the Scenes on *Big Wednesday*: Tales & Trivia from the Making of a Cult Classic,' *Wavelength Magazine*, online, 27 May, https://wavelengthmag.com/behind-the-scenes-big-wednesday-tales-trivia.

Geraghty, C. (2007) 'Re-Examining Stardom: Questions of Texts, Bodies and Performance,' in S. Redmond and S. Holmes (eds) *Stardom and Celebrity: A Reader*, Thousand Oaks, CA: Sage, pp. 98–110.

Gilbert, J. (1988) *A Cycle of Outrage: America's Reaction to the Juvenile Delinquent in the 1950s*, Oxford: Oxford University Press.

Gledhill, C. (1987) 'The Melodramatic Field: An Investigation,' in C. Gledhill (ed) *Home Is Where the Heart Is: Studies in Melodrama and the Women's Film*, London: British Film Institute, pp. 5–42.

Gray, J. (2010) *Show Sold Separately: Promos, Spoilers, and Other Media Paratexts*, New York, NY: New York University Press.

Green, T.H. (2013) 'John Milius: The Craziest Man in Hollywood?' *Telegraph*, online, 1 November, https://www.telegraph.co.uk/culture/film/film–news/10405943/John-Milius-the-craziest-man-in-Hollywood.html.

Grove, D. (2016) *Jan-Michael Vincent: The Edge of Greatness*, Sarasota, FL: BearManor Media.

Harkness, A. (2013) 'John Milius Is Just a Teddy Bear Toting an AK-47,' *Scotsman*, online, 1 November, https://www.scotsman.com/arts-and-culture/john-milius-just-teddy-bear-toting-ak-47-1554671.

Hay, J. (1990). '"You're Tearing Me Apart!": The Primal Scene of Teen Films,' *Cultural Studies*, Vol. 4, No. 3, pp. 331–338.

Hebdige, D. (1979) *Subculture: The Meaning of Style*, London: Routledge.

Henley, N.M. (1977) *Body Politics: Power, Sex and Non-verbal Communication*, Saddle River, NJ: Prentice Hall.

Hess, T.B. (1972) 'Pinup and Icon,' *Art News Annual*, Vol. 38, pp. 223–237.

Hills, M. (2013) 'Cult Movies with and without Cult Stars: Differentiating Discourses of Stardom,' in K. Egan and S. Thomas (eds) *Cult Film*

Stardom: Offbeat Attractions and Processes of Cultification, London: Palgrave Macmillan, pp. 21–36.

Howe, N. (2017) 'Seeds of a Surf Culture,' Surfer.com, online, 27 May, https://www.surfer.com/features/john-severson-interview.

Hunter, A. and Shearer, M. (2023) (eds) *Women and New Hollywood: Gender, Creative Labor, and 1970s American Cinema*. New Brunswick, NJ: Rutgers University Press.

Hutson, R. (2004) 'Sermons in Stone: Monument Valley in The Searchers,' in A.M. Eckstein and P.R. Lehman (eds) *The Searchers: Essays and Reflections on John Ford's Classic Western*, Detroit, MI: Wayne State University Press, pp. 93–108.

'International Box Office' (1978) *Screen International*, 22 July, p. 39.

Irwin, J.K. (1973) 'Surfing: The Natural History of an Urban Scene,' *Journal of Contemporary Ethnography* (formerly *Urban Life and Culture*) Vol. 2, No. 2, pp. 131–160.

Irwin, J.K. (1962) 'Surfers: A Study of the Growth of a Deviant Subculture,' Unpublished M.A. thesis, University of California–Berkeley.

Jackson, B. (2019) 'John Huston,' *Senses of Cinema*, No. 91, July, https://www.sensesofcinema.com/2019/great-directors/huston-john/.

Jancovich, M. (2010) 'Cult Fictions: Cult Movies, Subcultural Capital and the Production of Cultural Distinctions,' *Cultural Studies*, Vol. 16, No. 2, pp. 306–322.

Jeffords, S. (1993) 'The Big Switch: Hollywood Masculinity in the Nineties,' in J. Collins, H. Radner and A. Preacher Collins (eds) *Film Theory Goes to the Movies*, New York, NY: Routledge, pp. 196–208.

Kael, P. (1976) 'The Life and Times of Judge Roy Bean,' in *Reeling*, Boston, MA: Little, Brown.

Kampion, D. and Brown, B. (1998) *Stoked: A History of Surf Culture*, Beverly Hills, CA: Taschen.

Kapsis, R.E. (1989) 'Reputation Building and the Film Art World: The Case of Alfred Hitchcock,' *Sociological Quarterly*, Vol. 30, No. 1, Spring, pp. 15–35.

Kaser, B. (2013) '"Surfin'" Films: The Good, the Bad and the Wipeouts (Part 2: "Big Wednesday"),' Reel Life with Jane.com, online, 11 June, https://www.reellifewithjane.com/2013/06/surfin-films-the-good-the-bad-and-the-wipeouts-part-2-big-wednesday.

Kendrick, J. (2009) *Hollywood Bloodshed: Violence in 1980s American Cinema*, Carbondale, IL: Southern Illinois University Press.

Kerr, P. (1980) 'The Vietnam Subtext,' *Screen*, Vol. 21, No. 2, Summer, pp. 67–72.

King, G. (2002) *New Hollywood Cinema: An Introduction*. London: I.B. Tauris.

Klapp, O.E. (2014) *Heroes, Villains, and Fools: The Changing American Character*, Piscataway, NJ: Transaction.

Kohner, F. (1957) *Gidget: The Little Girl with Big Ideas*, Mountain View, CA: Ishi Press.

Krämer, P. (1999) 'A Powerful Cinema-going Force? Hollywood and Female Audiences since the 1960s,' in M. Stokes and R. Maltby (eds) *Identifying*

Hollywood's Audiences: Cultural Identifying and the Movies, London: British Film Institute, pp. 98–112.

Krämer, P. and Tzioumakis, Y. (2018) 'Introduction,' in P. Krämer and Y. Tzioumakis (eds) *The Hollywood Renaissance: Revisiting American Cinema's Most Celebrated Era*, New York, NY: Bloomsbury, pp. xiii–xxvii.

Laderman, S. (2014) *Empire in Waves: A Political History of Surfing*, Berkeley, CA: University of California Press.

Langford, B. (2007) '*American Graffiti* (1973),' in M. Merck (ed) *America First: Naming the Nation in US Film*, London: Routledge.

Lee, N. (2013) 'Milius,' *Film Threat*, online, 13 March, https://filmthreat.com/uncategorized/milius.

Leotta, Alfio (2018) *The Cinema of John Milius*, Lanham, MD: Lexington Books.

Lewis, J. (2003) 'The Perfect Money Machine(s): George Lucas, Steven Spielberg and Auteurism in the New Hollywood,' *Film International*, Vol. 1, No. 1, January, pp. 12–26.

Lindsey, R. (1978) 'The New New Wave of Film Makers: A Young Group of Writer-Directors Has Moved into Positions of Power in Hollywood,' *New York Times*, 28 May, p. SM3.

London, J. (2015) *Cruise of the Snark*, Scots Valley, CA: CreateSpace Independent Publishing Platform.

Loose, T. (2009) 'Interview with Greg MacGillivray,' *Coast Magazine*, online, 17 June, https://www.ocregister.com/2009/06/17/interview-with-greg-macgillivray/.

Lucas, G. (2013) Interviewed by Z. Knutson and J. Figueroa, in *Milius* [DVD], Paris, France: StudioCanal.

Lucas, G. and Spielberg, S. (2022) 'I Think I Found My People,' *Light and Magic*, Season 1, Episode 4, Disney+, 63 minutes.

Lutz, T. (2002) 'Men's Tears and the Roles of Melodrama,' in M. Shamir and J. Travis (eds) *Boys Don't Cry? Rethinking Narratives of Masculinity and Emotion in the U.S.*, New York, NY: Columbia University Press, pp. 185–204.

MacCabe, C. (1976) 'Theory and Film: Principles of Realism and Pleasure,' *Screen*, Vol. 17, No. 3, Autumn, pp. 7–28.

MacDonald, L.E. (2013) *The Invisible Art of Film Music: A Comprehensive History*, Lanham, MD: Scarecrow Press.

MacGillivray, G. (1978a) 'John Milius "Hangs Ten" on Film,' *American Cinematographer: International Journal of Motion Picture Photography and Production Techniques*, Vol. 59, No. 6, pp. 554–556, 572, 578, 608.

MacGillivray, G. (1978b) 'The Water Photography in Big Wednesday,' *American Cinematographer: International Journal of Motion Picture Photography and Production Techniques*, Vol. 59, No. 6, pp. 556–559, 580–582, 599–601, 610–613.

Mak, J. (2015) 'Creating "Paradise of the Pacific": How Tourism Began in Hawaii,' Working paper for the Economic Research Organization at the University of Hawaii, online, 3 February, https://uhero.hawaii.edu/RePEc/hae/wpaper/WP_2015-1.pdf.

Maloney, D.J. (2023) 'Lee Purcell on her role in "Big Wednesday", John Milius, and the "story underneath the story",' *The Weekly Show with David J. Maloney*, online, 4 August, https://www.youtube.com/watch?v=aM1Rz45Fmjw&ab_channel=TheWeeklyShowwithDavidJ.Maloney.

Marcus, B. (2020) 'Emotions of the Ocean: The *Big Wednesday* 20th Anniversary Reviewed,' Benmarcusrules.com, online, https://www.benmarcusrules.com/big-wednesday-book-review.

Maslin, J. (1978) 'Screen: "Big Wednesday" Gets Caught in Some Rough Surf: Buddyhood of Surfing,' *New York Times*, 28 July, p. C14.

Mathijs, E. and Sexton, J. (2011) *Cult Cinema: An Introduction*. Chichester, UK: Wiley Blackwell.

May, K.G. (2002) *Golden State, Golden Youth: The California Image in Popular Culture, 1955–1966*, Chapel Hill, NC: University of North Carolina Press.

McCrudden, M. (2016) 'Gary Busey – After They Were Famous,' YouTube, 18 January, https://www.youtube.com/watch?v=eIYKHsnr0IE&t=5s&ab_channel=BeforeTheyWereFamous.

McDonald, P. (2000) *The Star System: Hollywood's Production of Popular Identities*, New York, NY: Wallflower Press.

McGilligan, P. (1975) *James Cagney: The Actor as Auteur*, New York, NY: A. S. Barnes.

McInerney, P. (1979–1980) 'Apocalypse Then: Hollywood Looks Back at Vietnam,' *Film Quarterly*, Vol. 33, No. 2, Winter, pp. 21–32.

McKenna, M. (2020) *Nasty Business: The Marketing and Distribution of the Video Nasties*, Edinburgh: Edinburgh University Press.

McNally, K. (2013) 'Damaged Beauty: Montgomery Clift and the Redefinition of a Star Image' in K. Egan and S. Thomas (eds) *Cult Film Stardom: Offbeat Attractions and Processes of Cultification*, London: Palgrave Macmillan, pp. 181–196.

Medina, I.M.G. (2021) 'John Milius: The Right-Wing Filmmaker Blacklisted by Hollywood,' *El American*, online, 10 February, https://elamerican.com/john-milius-the-right-wing-filmmaker-vetoed-by-hollywood/.

Mercer, J. and Shingler, M. (2004) *Melodrama: Genre, Style, Sensibility*, New York, NY: Wallflower Press.

Moore, M.S. (2010) *Sweetness and Blood: How Surfing Spread from Hawaii and California to the Rest of the World with Some Unexpected Results*, New York, NY: Rodale Books.

Morris, G. (1993) 'Beyond the Beach: Social and Formal Aspects of AIP's Beach Party Movies,' *Journal of Popular Film and Television*, Vol. 21, No. 1, pp. 1–11.

Morrison, J. (2010) *Hollywood Reborn: Movie Stars of the 1970s*, New Brunswick, NJ: Rutgers University Press.

Moser, P. (2022) *Surf and Rescue: George Freeth and the Birth of California Beach Culture*, Champaign, IL: University of Illinois Press.

Moser, P. (2020) 'The Hawaii Promotion Committee and the Appropriation of Surfing,' *Pacific Historical Review*, Vol. 89, No. 4, pp. 500–527.

Murray, G. (2004) 'The Auteur as Star: Violence and Utopia in the Films of Sam Peckinpah,' in C. Henry and A. Ndalianis (eds) *Stars in Our Eyes: The Star Phenomenon in the Contemporary Era*, Westport, CT: Praeger, pp. 129–148.

Neale, S. (2000) *Genre and Hollywood*, London: Routledge.

Neale, S. (1995) 'Questions of Genre,' in B.K. Grant (ed) *Film Genre Reader II*, Austin, TX: University of Texas Press, pp. 159–183.

Nendel, J. (2009) 'Surfing in Early Twentieth-Century Hawai'i: The Appropriation of a Transcendent Experience to Competitive American Sport,' *International Journal of the History of Sport*, Vol. 26, No. 16, pp. 2432–2446.

'Newsgram' (1978) *The Independent Film Journal*, 2 June, p. 19.

Newsinger, J. (1993) '"Do You Walk the Walk?": Aspects of Masculinity in Some Vietnam War Films,' in P. Kirkham and J. Thumin (eds) *You Tarzan: Masculinity, Movies and Men*, London: Lawrence & Wishart, pp. 126–145.

O'Brian, K. (1995) 'Gidget: Surfing the Illusory Wave of Change,' *Popular Culture Review*, Vol. 6, No. 2, August, pp. 83–92.

Ombres, F. (2014) 'Small Screen Pick: Milius (EPIX, January 11),' *Film Comment*, Vol. 50, No. 1, January/February, p. 76.

Ormrod, J. (2005a) 'Endless Summer (1964): Consuming Waves and Surfing the Frontier,' *Film & History*, Vol. 35, No. 1, pp. 39–51.

Ormrod, J.M. (2005b) '"*Just the Lemon Next to the Pie*": Apocalypse, History and the Limits of Myth in *Big Wednesday*' (1978), *Scope: An On-line Journal of Film Studies*, https://www.nottingham.ac.uk/scope/documents/2005/february-2005/ormrod.pdf.

Parker, R. (2017) 'How "The Temple of Doom" Changed the MPAA Ratings System,' *Hollywood Reporter*, online, 23 May, https://www.hollywoodreporter.com/movies/movie-news/indiana-jones-temple-doom-changed-mpaa-ratings-system-999618/.

Pemberton, P.S. (2015) 'Hollywood Maverick John Milius Is More than Mere Eccentric, Friends Say,' *Tribune*, online, 14 April, available at: https://www.sanluisobispo.com/entertainment/movies-news-reviews/article39514776.html.

Peterson, A.T. and Dunworth, D.J. (2004) *Mythology in Our Midst: A Guide to Cultural References*, Westport, CT: Greenwood.

Purcell, L. (2022) 'Billy Katt and I Had so Much Fun Wednesday Night at the Big Wednesday Screening and Q/A at Tarantino's Theatre, the New Bev,' Facebook, 16 July, online, https://www.facebook.com/leepurcellfanpage/photos/a.10150166227719446/10160182371139446/?paipv=0&eav=AfZdKfvs35mHAu66EzilxH1G9VV7yM0aBo2o6M4w-blgHU5RXhpsm_kIWxBTXQDGbEU&_rdr.

Pye, M. and Myles, L. (1979) *The Movie Brats: How the Film Generation Took Over Hollywood*, London: Holt, Rinehart, and Winston.

'*Red Dawn*' (no date) *The Numbers*, online, https://the-numbers.com/movie/Red-Dawn#tab=box-office.

Riviere, F. (1979) 'Rebirth Nest: An Exclusive Interview with Francis Ford Coppola,' *L.A. Weekly*, 28 November, p. 40.

Russell, J. (2017) 'Producing the Spielberg "Brand",' in N. Morris (ed) *A Companion to Steven Spielberg*, Hoboken, NJ: John Wiley & Sons, pp. 45–57.

Ryan, M. and Kellner, D. (1990) *Camera Politica: The Politics and Ideology of Contemporary Hollywood Film*, Bloomington, IN: Indiana University Press.

Sarris, A. (2016) 'Notes on Auteur Theory in 1962,' in L. Braudy and M. Cohen (eds) *Film Theory and Criticism*, Oxford: Oxford University Press, pp. 585–588.

Savage, J. (2007) *Teenage: The Creation of Youth 1875–1945*, London: Faber.

Schatz, T. (1988) *The Genius of the System: Hollywood Filmmaking in the Studio Era*. Minneapolis, MN: University of Minnesota Press.

Schatz, T. (1981) *Hollywood Genres: Formulas, Filmmaking and the Studio System*, New York, NY: Random House.

Schrader, P. (1973) 'John Milius: Master of Flash,' *Los Angeles Weekly News*, 17 August, p. 26.

Scures, J. (1986) 'The Social Order of the Surfing World,' Doctoral thesis, University of Washington.

Segaloff, N. (2021) *Big Bad John: The John Milius Interviews*, Sarasota, FL: BearManor Media.

Segaloff, N. (2006) 'John Milius: The Good Fights,' in P. McGilligan (ed) *Backstory 4: Interviews with Screenwriters of the 1970s and 1980s*, Berkeley, CA: University of California Press, pp. 274–316.

Shary, T. (1997) 'The Teen Film and Its Methods of Study: A Book Review Essay,' *Journal of Popular Film and Television*, Vol. 25, No. 1, pp. 38–45.

Siebenand, P.A. (1975) 'The Beginnings of Gay Cinema in Los Angeles: The Industry and the Audience,' Unpublished Ph.D. thesis, University of Southern California.

Snider, B. (1973) 'Mr Macho,' *Esquire*, online, 1 June, https://classic.esquire.com/article/1973/6/1/mr-macho.

Stayton, R. (2006) 'A Barbarian Inside the Gates: Back to the Golden Rule Days with John Milius,' *Magazine of the Writers Guild of America, West*, online, October (archived from the original) https://web.archive.org/web/20131029040321/https://www.wga.org/writtenby/writtenbysub.aspx?id=2239.

Storey, J. (2009) 'Rockin' Hegemony: West Coast Rock and Amerika's War in Vietnam,' in J. Storey (ed) *Cultural Theory and Popular Culture: A Reader*, 4th edition, Harlow: Pearson, pp. 88–98.

Stranger, M. (2011) *Surfing Life: Surface, Substructure and the Commodification of the Sublime*, New York, NY: Routledge.

Stratton, J. (1997) 'On the Impossibility of Subcultural Origins,' in K. Gelder and S. Thorton (eds) *The Subcultures Reader*, London: Routledge, pp. 181–190.

Strongman, P. (1992) 'Waves of Cheer,' Film Reviews, *Vox*, No. 23, August, p. 88.

Subin, A.D. (2022) *Accidental Gods: On Race, Empire, and Men Unwittingly Turned Divine*, New York, NY: Metropolitan Books, pp. 359–377.

Symmons, T. (2016) *The New Hollywood Historical Film 1967–78*, Basingstoke: Palgrave Macmillan.

Synnott, A. (1987) 'Shame and Glory: A Sociology of Hair,' *British Journal of Sociology*, Vol. 38, No. 3, pp. 381–413.

Templer, E. (2006) *I'm no Angel: The Blonde in Fiction and Film*, Charlottesville, VA: University of Virginia Press.

Thomas, S.K. (2013) 'Marginal Moments of Spectacle: Character Actors, Cult Stardom and Hollywood Cinema,' in K. Egan and S. Thomas (eds) *Cult Film Stardom: Offbeat Attractions and Processes of Cultification*, Basingstoke: Palgrave Macmillan, pp. 37–56.

Thompson, R. (1976) 'Stoked,' *Film Comment*, Vol. 12, No. 4, July/August, p. 10.

Thorpe Jnr., R.W. and Bender, R. (2016) *Crow Killer: The Saga of Liver-Eating Johnson*, Bloomington: Indiana University Press.

Truffaut, F. (1954) 'Une certaine tendance dans le cinéma français' [A certain tendency in French cinema], *Cahiers du Cinéma*, No. 31, pp. 15–29. First published in English in *Cahiers du Cinema in English*, No. 1 (1966), pp. 31–41.

Tzioumakis, Y. (2006) 'Marketing David Mamet: Institutionally Assigned Film Authorship in Contemporary American Cinema,' *The Velvet Light Trap*, No. 57, Spring, pp. 60–75.

Variety staff (1977) 'Reviews: *Big Wednesday*,' *Variety*, online, 31 December, https://variety.com/1977/film/reviews/big-wednesday-1200424303/.

Vincent, J-M. (2007) *The Insider*, CBS, online, 18 September, https://www.youtube.com/watch?v=xeiFaFUWqZs&ab_channel=rcvheaven.

Waeber, J. (2018) 'Afterword: Looking Back at Rousseau's Pygmalion,' in K.G. Hambridge and J. Hicks (eds) *The Melodramatic Moment: Music and Theatrical Culture, 1790–1820*, Chicago, IL: University of Chicago Press, pp. 191–198.

Walker, B. (1973) 'Journals: LA,' *Film Comment*, Vol. 9, No. 4, July/August, pp. 2–3, 62–63.

Walker, I.H. (2011) *Waves of Resistance: Surfing and History in Twentieth-Century Hawai'i*, Honolulu, HI: University of Hawai'i Press.

Walsh, A.S. (1984) *Women's Film and Female Experience 1940–1950*, Hartford, CT: Praeger.

Warga, W. (1977) 'Milius Waxes Up 'Big Wednesday,' *Los Angeles Times*, 21 August, p. N7.

Warshaw, M. (2010) *The History of Surfing*, San Francisco, CA: Chronicle Books.

Weddle, D. (1994) *If They Move … Kill 'Em! The Life and Times of Sam Peckinpah*, New York, NY: Grove Press.

Weiler, A.H. (1973) 'The Screen: "Dillinger": Oates Plays Title Role in Film by Milius,' *New York Times*, 2 August, p. 31.

Wharton, D. (1995) 'BY DESIGN: Surf and Turf: It Seemed the Bear Belonged to No One – and Everyone. Then Director John Milius Decided His Logo Was Worth Fighting for,' *Los Angeles Times*, online, 28 September, https://www.latimes.com/archives/la-xpm-1995-09-28-ls-50870-story.html.

Wheaton, B. (2005) 'Selling Out? The Commercialisation and Globalisation of Lifestyle Sport,' in L. Allison (ed) *The Global Politics of Sport: The Role of Global Institutions in Sport*, London: Routledge, pp. 127–146.

White, G. (2023) 'Masculine Melodrama: How the "Male Weepie" Became Cinema's Go-to Genre,' *The National News*, online, 21 March, https://www.thenationalnews.com/arts-culture/film-tv/2023/03/21/film-masculine-melodrama-male-weepie/.

Williams, L. (1998) 'Melodrama Revised,' in N. Browne (ed) *Refiguring American Film Genres: History and Theory*, Berkeley, CA: University of California Press, pp. 42–88.

Windolf, J. (2008) 'Q&A Steven Spielberg,' *Vanity Fair*, online, 13 September, https://www.vanityfair.com/news/2008/02/spielberg_qanda200802.

Wojcik, P.R. (2021) *Gidget: Origins of a Teen Girl Transmedia Franchise*, London: Routledge.

Woodworth, A.J. (2014) 'From Buddy Film to Bromance: Masculinity and Male Melodrama Since 1969,' Doctoral thesis, Temple University.

Wright, J.L. (2016) 'The all-American Golden Boy: Robert Redford, Blond Hair and Masculinity in Hollywood,' *Celebrity Studies*, Vol. 7, No. 1, pp. 69–82.

Wyatt, J. (1994) *High Concept: Movies and Marketing in Hollywood*, Austin, TX: University of Texas Press.

Index

Note: Page numbers followed by 'n' refer to end notes.

1941 6, 9, 14n2, 15
Aaberg, Dennis 1, 16, 65, 107, 110
Addiction 87, 96, 103–105, 107
Ageing, inevitability of 16, 20, 21, 24
Airwolf (1984–6) 87, 103
American Graffiti (1973) 6, 8, 72, 81, 85, 86n3, 110–112
American International Pictures (AIP) 2, 39–4 0, 50, 56
American Screenwriters Guild, The 66
Antunes, Filipa 10–1 1
Apocalypse Now (1979) 5, 71, 72
Archetypes 36, 91–9 5
Authenticity 14, 40, 42, 44, 49, 50, 52, 59, 61, 108, 111–112
Auteurism, general (see also, Milius, John as brand) 55, 60, 68n1, 74, 82, 85

Bart, Peter 13
Battle for Algiers (1966) 13
Beach Boys, The 39, 41, 50
Beach Party movies 2, 36, 39–41, 50
Bear (character in *Big Wednesday*) 18, 19, 21–22, 24–28, 32–33
Bear (brand) 50–5 2, 112n1
Big Lebowski, The (1998) 6
Biskind, Peter 8, 54–55
Blacker, Irwin 17
Blacklist 6–7
Blockbuster era 10
Bolton, Lucy 109
Booth, Douglass 40, 42–44, 46, 49
Branding (see also Milius, John, as auteur, as brand) 10, 36, 46, 49, 55, 67
Brown, Bruce 33, 42, 45
Burtt, Ben 8
Busey, Gary 3, 87–88, 90–91, 95–98, 101, 106–109

Camera Politica 23
Canby, Vincent 15n6, 56
Captain Cook 44–45
Character actors 27, 87, 96
Clift, Montgomery 105, 108
Close Encounters of the Third Kind (1977) 7–9
Coca-Cola 50, 52
Coming-of-age drama 1, 26, 35, 78, 108
Conan the Barbarian (1982) 6, 69, 76, 83
Coppola, Francis Ford 5, 54, 63, 67, 68n1, 80
Corrigan, Timothy 3, 55–56, 59–61, 66
Cox, Alex 110
Cult of personality 56, 61, 63, 68n3

Dante, Joe 11
Dean, James 40, 91, 95, 102, 105, 108
De Palma, Brian 5, 60, 75
Dillinger (1973) 6, 57, 58, 69
Directors Guild of America (DGA) 11
Dirty Harry (1971) 5, 27, 84
Distribution, DVD and Blu-ray 80, 83–84
Doherty, Thomas 38–3 9

Dubbert, Joe 74
Duval, Robert 5
Dyer, Richard 59, 60, 89, 90, 91–93, 94

Eastwood, Clint 5, 93
Edison, Thomas 46, 48
Egan, Kate 88–89
Endless Summer (1966) 33, 42
Excess 6, 13, 29, 53, 61, 63, 73, 75–76, 77, 82–83, 85, 88, 89, 91, 95–98, 107–109
Exhibition, theatrical 2, 8, 80, 84

Fetty, Darrell 106
Fisher, Carrie 8
Ford, Alexander Hume 45–47
Ford, Harrison 8, 89, 102–103
Ford, John 1, 5, 27, 30, 32, 35, 58
Foucault, Michel 55
Frames as thresholds 30–33
Freeth, George 47–48
Freytag, Gustav 17–19

Genre 2, 3, 4, 11, 38, 42, 65, 69–73, 84–85, 106, 111
Geraghty, Christine 89
Gidget (1959) 39–41
Gledhill, Christine 73–74, 85n1
Good Joe, The 92–93, 98–102
Grandiose and/or pretentious 1, 2, 28, 76–77, 110
Great men 1, 58
Greatest American Hero, The (1981–1983) 87, 98–99, 102
Gremlins (1984) 11–12, 15n6
Grove, David 102–106

Haig, General Alexander 12–13
Hale, Barbara 20, 99
Hamill, Mark 8, 100
Hamilton, Billy 50–51
Hawaii 3, 45, 47–48
Hawai'i Promotion Committee, The (HPC) 37, 45–48
Hawks, Howard 5
Hebdige, Dick 42–43
Hemmingway, Ernest 64, 93
Hills, Matt 88–90
Hitchcock, Alfred 65–66, 98
Hollywood Show, The 105–106

How Green Was My Valley (1941) 1
Hudson Institute, The 12–13
Huston, John 5, 29, 56
Huyck, Willard 8, 14n2

Indiana Jones and the Temple of Doom (1984) 9, 10, 11–12
Intergenerational conflict 20, 24

Jan and Dean 2, 39, 41
Jaws (1975) 5, 8, 9, 12
Jeremiah Johnson (1972) 13, 56
Jingoism 12–13
JIP Inc. 51–52
Juvenile delinquency 36–39

Kael, Pauline 56–59
Kahanamoku, Duke 48–49
Kapsis, Robert E. 3, 59, 65–66
Katt, William 70, 81, 84, 87–88, 90–91, 92, 98–102, 106, 108–109
Katz, Gloria 8
Katzenberg, Jeffrey 9, 61
Klapp, Orrin Edgar 91–95
Kleiser, Randal 65, 67
Krämer, Peter 78

Leotta, Alfio 6–7, 8, 13, 29, 55, 67
Lewis, Jon 68n1
Life and Times of Judge Roy Bean, The (1972) 56
Lobalzo Wright, Julie 100–101, 109
London, Jack 48
Lord of the Flies (1954) 12
Lucas, George 5–8, 9–11, 14, 15n5, 28, 54, 60, 63, 65, 67, 68n1, 72, 86n3, 111
Lutz, Tom 74

MacGillivray, Greg 28, 29, 33–35, 49, 65
Malibu 1, 16, 39, 40, 51
Marketing 70–71, 81–82
Mathijs, Ernest 82–83, 85, 88, 102, 105, 107–108
McDonald, Paul 95
McNally, Karen 105
Melodrama 70–72
  Male melodrama 69–70, 74–76, 78–82
  The Woman's Film 70, 73–77, 85

Mercer, John 73, 77
Milius, John
  As auteur 3, 11, 29, 54–56, 58–60, 63, 65–66
  As brand 3, 13, 17, 53–54, 61–65
  As star 56–61
  In crisis 65–67
  As *Enfant terrible* 6, 57
Monroe, Marilyn 49, 105, 108
Movie moguls 9, 11
Motion Picture Association of America (MPAA) 11, 14
Movie Brats, The 5, 72
Movie ratings 10–12
Moviedrome (1988–2000) 110
Myth 2, 26–29, 32, 33, 35, 59, 64, 65, 76

National Lampoon's Animal House (1978) 29, 81, 111
Neale, Steve 70, 72, 73
New Beverly Cinema, The 2, 84
New Hollywood, The, 4, 5, 7, 9, 54–55, 68n1, 72, 111
Newsinger, John 75–76
No Pants Mance (1973) 16
Nostalgia 8, 32, 80, 85n2, 111, 112
Novelisation 16, 111

Ormrod, Joan 42, 71

Peckinpah, Sam 16, 25, 35, 58, 63–64, 67, 83, 103
Peralta, Stacy 47
Performativity 3, 56–5 9, 61, 62
Persona 3, 6–7, 10, 12, 15n5, 53–54, 56–59
PG-13 10–12
Pitch letter 110
Poledouris, Basil 76–77
Poltergeist (1982) 11–1 2, 15n6
Pretentious and/or grandiose 1, 2, 28, 76–77, 110
Production of *Big Wednesday* 2, 7–9, 13, 33–35, 81–82
Profit participation points 7–9, 14
Purcell, Lee 71, 84, 106
"Pure" surfing films 42, 46

Quigg, Joe 49

Raiders of the Lost Ark (1981) 14, 15n4
Rambo 12, 75
Rebel without a Cause (1955) 3, 38, 40, 73, 82, 85, 95
Red Dawn (1984) 6, 10, 12–14, 69, 83
Reputation-building 65–67
Reversal of Richard Sun, The (1970) 76
Reynolds, Burt 102, 105
Reynolds, Kevin 12
Roosevelt, Theodore 53, 58

Sarris, Andrew 55
Saturday Night Fever (1977) 8, 80
Saving Private Ryan (1998) 9
Schrader, Paul 5, 57–58
Score, musical 76–77
Scorsese, Martin 5, 57, 68n1, 72
Searchers, The (1956) 27, 30, 32
Severson, John 16, 35n1, 41
Sexton, Jamie
  82–83, 85, 88, 102, 105, 107–108
Shakespeare, William 17
Schatz, Thomas 55, 73–74,
Shaw, Robert 5
Shingler, Martin 73, 77
Siebenand, Paul Alcuin 103
Snider, Burr 6, 58
Spielberg, Steven 5–12, 14, 15n4, 15n6, 54, 60, 63, 65, 67, 68n1, 110
Spirit of comradeship 8, 14, 75
Sport 3, 16, 33, 36–37, 39, 41, 44, 49–50
Staiger, Janet 95
Star Wars (1977) 7–10, 15n5, 28, 89–90, 100, 103
Stardom
  As construction 56–61, 63–65
  Cult stardom 88–91, 102, 103, 105–108
  Inconsistencies 59–61, 64–65
  Youthful types 87–88, 90–91
Storey, John 43
Style (film) 29, 32–35
Surfing
  As Olympic sport 37
  Commercialisation of 37, 42, 45, 49, 52
  History of 44–49
Surfing boom 37, 39–40
Surf Nazis 40–41
Symbolism 27, 32–33
Synnott, Anthony 100

Tarantino, Quentin 84, 110
Teenagers 38–40, 70, 72, 85n2, 87, 101, 102, 103
Teen films 3, 38, 70
Templer, Ellen 100
Thomas, Sarah 88–89, 96
Tourism 3, 37, 46–48
Tragic hero 73, 87, 102–107, 108
Truffaut, François 55
Tzioumakis, Yannis 60, 78

University of Southern California (USC) 14n2, 17, 63, 65, 76

Valenti, Jack 12
Vietnam War 6, 18, 19, 22, 23–24, 71–72, 75, 80, 111
Vincent, Jan-Michael 71, 87–88, 90–92, 95, 102–107, 108–109

Warner Bros. 51, 56, 71, 81–82, 83, 84
Wild Bunch, The (1969) 25
Williams, Linda 73–75, 78
Wojcik, Pamela Robertson 40
Wong, Kar-Wai 32
Woman's film, The (see Melodrama)
Woodworth, Amy J. 80–81

Yablans, Frank 13
Youthful abandon 20

Zanuck, Darrylin 49
Zahn, Tommy 49
Zoetrope Studios 54

For Product Safety Concerns and Information please contact our EU
representative GPSR@taylorandfrancis.com
Taylor & Francis Verlag GmbH, Kaufingerstraße 24, 80331 München, Germany

www.ingramcontent.com/pod-product-compliance
Lightning Source LLC
LaVergne TN
LVHW010926110826
845149LV00013B/2491
9781032801117